"If the most trusted person you know handed you the deed to a property where he had discovered a rich vein of gold, would you mind getting your hands dirty and making the necessary changes in your life to harvest this amazing gift? Most of us would certainly not. And yet we often sit idly by in the face of equally amazing opportunities, wasting our lives in the prison of comfortable predictability.

This might well be the answer to this age-old question: 'How stupid can you get?'

In *Letting God's Word Speak: Lessons on Deepening Your Faith*, Tony Crouch has created a supernatural passport to transport you into a life of incomparable joy and productivity. He is handing you tools to harvest those 'gold' opportunities and never miss another encounter of blessing and vision.

This book will give you a deep and dynamic understanding of the fullness of God's grace and will unleash His ability in your life. It is not a brief poof of feel-good read but an inspired collection of divine frequencies to set you on the path your heart has been longing for.

Get ready to go high and go deep with *Letting God's Word Speak: Lessons on Deepening Your Faith*."

—Len Mink,
Len Mink Ministries

"*Letting God's Word Speak: Lessons on Deepening Your Faith* is an invitation to consider how God not only calls us but calls us forward in active relationship. Steeped in scripture and personal stories, Tony Crouch's book shares openly about his relationship with God in order to encourage others on their faith journeys. Everyone needs a friend to encourage them in the faith, and while reading this book, you can't help but let Tony become your encourager, teacher, and friend."

—Rev. Molly Just,
Campus Minister, Director of Discipleship,
Southwestern College, Winfield, Kansas

LETTING
GOD'S WORD
SPEAK

———❖———

LESSONS ON DEEPENING YOUR FAITH

TONY CROUCH

CLAY BRIDGES
PRESS

TABLE OF CONTENTS

SPECIAL THANKS

I wrote this book at the insistence of my good friend and prayer partner Herlynda "Lynne" (Jordan) Fisher. I met Lynne about 25 years ago and soon found a strong mutual interest in faith. We've shared both our prayer requests and our praises over those inspiring times when God was most visible in our lives. Anytime you ask Lynne about her day, she always responds, "It's all good!" What's more, she means it. Her faith prepares her to face each new day with excitement and courage. She has often carried God's words to my ears. She truly hears God and acts on what she hears. She's never ended a conversation without adding, "Don't forget; I'm praying for you." And I for you, Miss Lynne. Thank you!

Of course, no person is who they are without their family and friends. I'm fortunate that my parents have always supported me in my endeavors. They challenged and encouraged me. Much credit for my good qualities goes to them. They made sure I was raised on the good news of Jesus, took me to church every time the door was open, and gave me a desire to grow more deeply in my relationship with God.

My wife, Vicki, is the love of my life. From day one, she has been patient with me, helping me grow and mature as a person and a Christian. She is the strongest person I know. No matter how much I study and grow, I will probably never reach the level of relationship she has with Jesus. She never compromises her faith, always stands her ground, and usually voices her opinions, even when I don't want to hear them. I won't say every day has been easy. We have disagreed occasionally. (Don't ever ask us to do a home improvement project together!) But we have never ended a day angry with each other. I can't imagine where I would be today without her.

Through my kids and grandkids, I have learned unconditional love. We've tried each other's patience and disagreed over direction and decisions, but we've always been there for one another. If and when I need something, I know they will be first in line to help. But more than that, their individual compassion for those around them is amazing. They care about people. I love each of them.

Thank you to all my friends and coworkers throughout the years. I've learned from each of you.

Family and friends aside, this book is dedicated to our supreme God in his three distinct but equal characters—Father, Son, and Holy Spirit. The words of this book are his.

> *All things were made through him. Without him, nothing was made that has been made. In him was life, and the life was the light of men. The light shines in the darkness, and the darkness hasn't overcome it.*
>
> —John 1:3–5

INTRODUCTION

This book started one evening when I was watching a TV show about evangelism. In a very clear voice, I heard God say, "You need to start a Facebook page for me." Facebook was a big leap for me. I didn't mind sharing my testimony and thoughts on the Bible, but using Facebook was extremely out of character. But on that Facebook post, Herlynda Fisher wrote in a comment, "Are you writing a book? I believe more people should benefit from the anointed words from our Lord via you. Please stay obedient to His Word." Of course, my first reaction was "No way." But as I considered her comment, I pondered this: "If you believe you are led by the Holy Spirit, this isn't yours. Why wouldn't you think he would want you to share it?" During a phone call, I told her I was considering a book, and she said, "It's about his Word!" So here we are. This book is about the Bible, my faith journey, and the grace I've lived.

What qualifies me to do this? Nothing qualifies me that doesn't also qualify each of you who believe in and surrender to Jesus as your Lord and Savior. The Holy Spirit led me to record the words. Of course, the words come from my life experience and are in my Okie dialect. I have endeavored to balance my opinion with scripture.

A few basic beliefs underpin this book. First, the Holy Bible is God's Spirit talking to our spirits. Because of this, we have to believe the Holy Bible as written, in context, and taken as a whole. To take the Word as a whole means we have to know the Word as a whole, and that means reading and studying it for ourselves. The love of the Father is consistent throughout. The tree of life is mentioned in Genesis 3 and Revelation 22—

the beginning and the end. It was always God's plan that we would spend eternity with him.

The second basic belief that builds on the first is found in Genesis 1:1: *"In the beginning, God created the heavens and the earth."* This verse is the basic tenet of my belief. Without God as the Creator, the whole of our relationship with God has no meaning, and this exercise is futile. John 1:1–5 says, *"In the beginning was the Word, and the Word was with God, and the Word was God. The same was in the beginning with God. All things were made through him. Without him, nothing was made that has been made. In him was life, and the life was the light of men. The light shines in the darkness, and the darkness hasn't overcome it."* Simply put, the existence of God in three realities—Father, Son, and Spirit—has always been. Jesus was always with God, and then he came to show us the way with a light that will never go out. Jesus was there in the beginning, and he will be there in the end. *"I am the Alpha and the Omega, the First and the Last, the Beginning and the End"* (Rev. 22:13).

The second belief leads directly to the third. *"Jesus said to him, 'I am the way, the truth, and the life. No one comes to the Father, except through me. If you had known me, you would have known my Father also. From now on, you know him, and have seen him'"* (John 14:6–7). It can't be said any simpler. In John 14–16, Jesus prepares his disciples for his death on the cross. Through his willingness to take all our sins on the cross, we gained salvation. Salvation doesn't come from being nice or loving our neighbor. It is an act of God's grace through Jesus. Our only requirement is to repent, accept it, and receive it.

We all should know what we believe and why we believe it. If anything in this book makes you stop and ponder your knowledge of and relationship with Jesus, we will have met our goal together.

A CONVERSATION I HAVEN'T BEEN
ABLE TO GET OFF MY MIND

God created man in his own image. In God's image he created him; male and female he created them.

—Gen. 1:27

But Yahweh said to Samuel, "Don't look on his face, or on the height of his stature, because I have rejected him; for I don't see as man sees. For man looks at the outward appearance, but Yahweh looks at the heart."

—I Sam. 16:7

Don't judge according to appearance, but judge righteous judgment.

—John 7:24

A new commandment I give to you, that you love one another. Just as I have loved you, you also love one another. By this everyone will know that you are my disciples, if you have love for one another.

—John 13:34–35

For there is no partiality with God.

—Rom. 2:11

Recently, I checked in with a friend about his wife who had been in the hospital. His answer to my question still bothers me today. He said, "Well, she's home, and I'm glad for that, but I'm just frustrated. This is just how life treats us."

I asked him to explain.

"I took her to the first hospital because she needed attention," he explained. "They figured out what was wrong. Next thing I knew, they took out the directions for the machine they were trying to hook her up to. After a small procedure and a couple of hours, they suggested she be moved to a specialized hospital. We made that move the same day. At the other hospital, they put her in a room. There she lay for four days. At some point, they decided to check the bandage on the incision that was part of the procedure at the first hospital. That's when they found out the incision was four times larger than needed and was contributing to her issue. It was a comedy from there—lost paperwork, miscommunication. But I should expect that. It's just how life treats me."

I asked what he meant.

"Oh, it's my appearance. I don't go out to eat because they bring me other people's leftover food, or it has plastic pieces or hair in it. I took her to the other hospital because the closest one had once refused to treat me for a spider bite because they assumed I was a druggie."

My stunned silence prompted him to continue.

"I went one time to buy supplies for my employer. When I tried to check out, I was told there was a problem with our business account. I called the office and was assured the account was fine. I told the sales clerk, and he said, 'Nope, there is clearly a problem with the account.' When I got back to the office, someone told me the store called after I left and said, 'Some thug was here trying to charge to your account. We told him there was a problem. Just thought you would like to know.' Oh, by the way, did I mention I was wearing a company uniform, had my employee badge, and was driving a company truck?"

I obviously knew this guy. He was unconventional—doesn't look like me or maybe even you. My experiences with him suggest that if human

4

beings were to look on the heart, they would see someone just trying to love others.

Where are we as a society? Has society shifted in such a way that we can't tolerate what's different—and I don't just mean appearance or skin color. I hear people say, "I don't want to go if so-and-so is going to be there. I just don't agree with them." Okay, but what about dialogue? Can we no longer discuss and accept someone for their opinions, even if we don't agree? Since God created us in his image, since we are commanded to love one another, since God looks on the heart, how should we react to stories like this?

I'm struggling on two fronts. First, how do we regain civility? How do we get the word out that God intends for us to look on the heart and not outward appearances?

Second, and more importantly, how can I see as God sees and share that perspective with my downtrodden friend? I told him I was amazed at the responses he received, that they clearly weren't right. But what can I do that is more tangible?

The answer goes back to my call to write this book. I can share with others what the Holy Spirit has taught me through prayer and study.

WHAT'S
YOUR STORY?

Give thanks to Yahweh, for he is good, for his loving kindness endures forever. Let the redeemed by Yahweh say so, whom he has redeemed from the hand of the adversary.

—Ps. 107:1–2

Neither do you light a lamp and put it under a measuring basket, but on a stand; and it shines to all who are in the house. Even so, let your light shine before men, that they may see your good works and glorify your Father who is in heaven.

—Matt. 5:15–16

Then he said to his disciples, "The harvest indeed is plentiful, but the laborers are few. Pray therefore that the Lord of the harvest will send out laborers into his harvest."

—Matt. 9:37–38

Jesus came to them and spoke to them, saying, "All authority has been given to me in heaven and on earth. Go and make disciples of all nations, baptizing them in the name of the Father and of the Son and of the Holy Spirit, teaching them to observe all things that I commanded you. Behold, I am with you always, even to the end of the age." Amen.

—Matt. 28:18–20

A few years ago, I was in a group called People of the Covenant, a weekly study of the Holy Bible. But more than study, it taught the participants how to tell their stories. I've heard a few great messages on sharing the Word, and all center on one thing—telling *your* story. No one can argue with the facts of your story and the impact of Jesus in your life. It is your story. It isn't controversial. And guess what? You don't have to study to remember the details. I challenge each of you who might read this to share your story and what God has taught you or done for you. Somewhere in our vast experiences, we will speak to someone who is looking for Jesus.

I'll start with my story.

I must acknowledge that I was privileged as a child. I grew up in a Christian home with great role models, and I assume those influences are why my life has gone the direction it has. My folks were, and still are, deeply committed to Christ's values. Some of my oldest memories are of "extended session" (kid's church) at First Christian Church in Alva, Oklahoma. The names of some of the ladies who taught us are fading, but the faces and stories remain—Noah and the Ark, Adam and Eve, Zacchaeus and the tree, Abraham and Sarah, Moses. I also remember those who I thought sat with God for supper—elders in our church who were examples and mentors of a Christ-centered life. I remember Sunday school teachers who taught us how to grow our own knowledge and not just live off someone else's faith. And then there was Bob, the church custodian. He was the kindest, gentlest person I can remember from my youth. He let us get in his way and keep him from getting things done, but he always turned our time with him into a lesson about Jesus. He played Santa at Christmas, and all he really needed was the suit. Bob was just Bob, an amazing example of Christ's love.

As you can see, my childhood was built around church. We were always there. When I was 10, our minister offered a membership class for those in the fourth through sixth grades, as was the custom each spring. The class culminated in our joining church and being baptized on

Mother's Day, 1974. Joining was a natural decision for me. I don't have a miraculous conversion story.

God was always there for me, and without really understanding how or why, I always felt so in the back of my mind. I know of countless times when the Holy Spirit was with me as I made decisions. For example, I'm an accountant by trade. I wanted to get out of industry and into higher education where I thought my skills could have more meaning. When I found the right fit and was offered a job, the pay didn't fit. As much as I wanted that job, I couldn't take it. About four months later, I received a phone call with another offer for the job. This time, the money worked. All the other candidates had needed the same amount of pay I did to take the job. The person who would be my boss told me, "If I was going to have to pay that amount anyway, I thought I might as well go back to the person I want." God had worked it out so the job fit my needs, but he also taught me a lesson in patience and trust in the process. Sometimes, what I saw as missed opportunities were God's protection.

Over the years, I've been a church custodian, bus driver, choir member, committee member, committee chair, treasurer, deacon, elder, trustee, and board moderator. I've helped rewrite policies and bylaws and set up endowments. When it comes to "doing" church, I've just about done it all.

I have also led Sunday school classes and studies on and off since I was in college. I like doing it because it forces me to go deeper into God's Word. I've always excelled in the academic function of my relationship with God. I've long had the sense that God wanted to use me for something, I guess because I've sensed him with me protecting me. I assumed that doing church was what God wanted. I'll admit that it kept me busy.

My amazing wife, Vicki, and our kids, grandkids, and great-grandkids keep me inspired. Vicki is the exact opposite of me spiritually. Where I want to know, she wants to feel. Through her, I've learned that it's great to have a strong intellectual background in the Word, but truly being a follower of Christ is not just an academic exercise. There has to be a human connection, and that means feelings.

I've become much more intentional about hearing God's voice, not just counting on him to be there as he always has been. Along the way, I've realized that something was missing in my relationship with God. It was surrender—or a lack thereof. It started by listening to others' experiences. If I wanted to go deeper in my relationship, I needed to surrender. This endeavor that began on Facebook was a step for me, but it exploded recently with an invitation to join a journey called Spiritual Direction (I'll talk more about that in a later chapter). Accepting that invitation was the springboard to surrendering my will to his in new and profound ways, not the least of which is using a prayer language.

Surrender requires trust. I've always been a planner who wants to know steps A–Z before I begin a journey. God wants us to look to him and trust him. In surrendering my will, I have to accept that even without knowing step two, God wants me to take step one and trust him. Trust leads to peace. I have a new peace around me that I have never experienced, and it is amazing. *"And the peace of God, which surpasses all understanding, will guard your hearts and your thoughts in Christ Jesus"* (Phil. 4:7).

In a Bible study, our group was discussing the forms of God's grace—the dramatic saving grace and the sustaining keeping grace. Both forms are amazing, and both cost the exact same price—Jesus's life.

> *But now apart from the law, a righteousness of God has been revealed, being testified by the law and the prophets; even the righteousness of God through faith in Jesus Christ to all and on all those who believe. For there is no distinction, for all have sinned, and fall short of the glory of God.*
>
> —Rom. 3:21–23

It hasn't all been easy. I've made my share of mistakes, and I'm nowhere near God's destination for me. But I'm moving, and I'm an example of his keeping grace. It has sustained me for all my years and does so even more today.

Jesus calls us to acknowledge him, to have an intimate relationship with him. He calls us to share our story. He tells us that his harvest is ready, but the laborers are few. He tells us to go. He tells us he is with us wherever we go. Are you ready, willing, and able to be a laborer for Jesus?

Our story is our relationship with God. What's your story?

---◆---

HOW CAN
THIS POSSIBLY BE?

An angel of the Lord appeared to him, standing on the right side of the altar of incense. Zacharias was troubled when he saw him, and fear fell upon him. But the angel said to him, "Don't be afraid, Zacharias, because your request has been heard. Your wife, Elizabeth, will bear you a son, and you shall call his name John. You will have joy and gladness, and many will rejoice at his birth. For he will be great in the sight of the Lord, and he will drink no wine nor strong drink. He will be filled with the Holy Spirit, even from his mother's womb."

—Luke 1:11–15

Zacharias said to the angel, "How can I be sure of this? For I am an old man, and my wife is well advanced in years."

—Luke 1:18

The angel said to her, "Don't be afraid, Mary, for you have found favor with God. Behold, you will conceive in your womb and give birth to a son, and shall name him 'Jesus.'"

—Luke 1:30–31

Mary said to the angel, "How can this be, seeing I am a virgin?"

—Luke 1:34

For nothing spoken by God is impossible.

—Luke 1:37

We tend to be a bit surprised by both Zechariah's and Mary's responses to the angel's announcements. We think, "You mean you saw an angel right in front of you and questioned *how*?" But with the knowledge of scripture and history, we do the same thing. We don't think we're worthy of God's favor. (Well, we aren't; Jesus made us worthy.) I'm not necessarily talking about grand events, though I believe there are grand events (miracles) today. I'm talking about small events that happen day to day that we question.

Recently, one of my coworkers asked me whether I would accept a favor. I thought it a strange question, so I said, "Possibly." She asked if she could have my keys because her husband wanted to wash my truck. If you had seen my truck that day, you would know how grand a gesture her offer really was. My stunned question was, "Why in the world would he want to wash my truck?" "Just because" was all I got back in return. Too busy to argue with her, I handed her my keys and said, "I have to go to Oklahoma City at 11:00." She said, "Won't it feel good to do it in a clean truck?"

At about one minute to 11:00, she handed me my keys, and with a huge smile said, "Enjoy!" When I went out to the parking lot, all I could do was cry (old age has made the seals in my eyes leak a bit). I opened the truck door and found that the inside had been cleaned as well. I called her cell phone. No answer. I tried to leave a message, but I'm not sure she could understand much of it. I was overwhelmed. My mind was still trying to grasp a reason for this incredible, special gift. A few minutes later, I received a text from her: "Thank you for allowing us the opportunity to bless you!"

Think about that for a minute. How many blessings does God try to send our way, but we miss them because we analyze them to death? How can this possibly be? Why in the world would you want to do that? I'm still amazed at this wonderful gift. I'm still amazed at the wonderful life God has allowed me to live. How can this possibly be? Why in the world would he want to do that for me? Maybe because of this: "*For God so loved the world, that he gave his one and only Son, that whoever believes in him should not perish, but have eternal life*" (John 3:16).

❖

IS YOUR
RADIO ON?

You will keep whoever's mind is steadfast in perfect peace, because he trusts in you. Trust in Yahweh forever; for in Yah, Yahweh, is an everlasting Rock.

—Isa. 26:3–4

The gatekeeper opens the gate for him, and the sheep listen to his voice. He calls his own sheep by name, and leads them out. Whenever he brings out his own sheep, he goes before them, and the sheep follow him, for they know his voice.

—John 10:3–4

I'm a country music fan, especially a good ol' country gospel song. You may have heard the country gospel hit "Turn Your Radio On" written by Albert Brumley in 1939. The Statler Brothers and Ray Stevens both sang great versions of the song. Musically, I have to give the edge to the Statler Brothers. Who can resist the rich bass of the late Harold Reid or the incredible tenor of Jimmy Fortune, along with the harmonies of Don Reid and Phil Balsley? But theologically, I give the edge to Ray Stevens. The verses he includes bring the song more into perspective for me.

When I was younger (okay, much younger), I loved the song, but I never understood why I couldn't get God when I listened to the radio. I changed the stations, but in Alva you could really only pick up KALV, and God never spoke from 1430 AM that I heard. As I've matured a bit and grown somewhat wiser, the lyrics have taken on a special meaning for me. They imply that God is a radio station and we are radios that need to be turned on.

As the passage from Isaiah says, God keeps us in peace when we are steadfast in him. John reminds us that Jesus, our Good Shepherd, knows each of us and calls us by name. When we hear him, we follow. But what about when we don't hear him? Whose fault is it if we can't hear Jesus's voice? The radio station is always broadcasting (most are now 24-hour stations), but if we don't have the radio on, we won't hear a thing. If we have the radio on but it isn't tuned to the correct frequency, we won't hear what we need to hear. In fact, we might hear things we don't want to hear or don't need to hear. Like a radio station, God is always love, always calling us to follow him through the Holy Spirit. If we can't hear His voice, you can bet it's because we are turned off or tuned in to the wrong thing.

I've lost a little weight lately, and the simple method is to drink more water. The more water I put in, the less room there is for food. I've found a correlation in God's Word. The more of God's Word I put in (through private devotions, group study of the Holy Bible, Christian TV, country gospel music, and so forth), the less room I have for junk (and the stuff of the world *is* junk). I may not be quite as informed in worldly things, but I'm a hundred times more content in the Rock who is my peace.

My questions to you are these: What do you spend your free time listening to? Are you letting God in through your ears? What do you spend your free time watching? Are you letting God in through your eyes? What do you spend your free time doing? Are you letting God in through your thoughts and actions? If you're not letting God in, if your radio is off or tuned to the wrong station, I'm betting that you're allowing too much of yourself to be occupied by the world and not enough by God's peace. Is your radio tuned in to God's broadcast frequency?

---❖---

WHAT WAS
THE QUESTION?

That the God of our Lord Jesus Christ, the Father of glory, may give to you a spirit of wisdom and revelation in the knowledge of him, having the eyes of your hearts enlightened, that you may know what is the hope of his calling, and what are the riches of the glory of his inheritance in the saints, and what is the exceeding greatness of his power toward us who believe, according to that working of the strength of his might.

—Eph. 1:17–19

He awoke, and rebuked the wind, and said to the sea, "Peace! Be still!" The wind ceased, and there was a great calm. He said to them, "Why are you so afraid? How is it that you have no faith?"

—Mark 4:39–40

I am the vine. You are the branches. He who remains in me and I in him bears much fruit, for apart from me you can do nothing. If a man doesn't remain in me, he is thrown out as a branch and is withered; and they gather them, throw them into the fire, and they are burned. If you remain in me, and my words remain in you, you will ask whatever you desire, and it will be done for you. In this my Father is glorified, that you bear much fruit; and so you will be my disciples.

—John 15:5–8

Be subject therefore to God. Resist the devil, and he will flee from you.

—James 4:7

So faith comes by hearing, and hearing by the word of God.

—Rom. 10:17

Who was baseball's World Series champion the year you were born? Who won the Heisman Trophy nine years ago? Who has the most All-Around Championship awards for cowboys? What was the closing number of the New York Stock Exchange yesterday? What are the angles in a right triangle? What is Harry Potter best known for?

How about these questions: Who was Jesus's relative who was struck mute in the temple? What was Moses's father-in-law's name? How many years did Jacob work to receive Rachel as his wife? What did God create on the second day? What is the fifth commandment? What is the greatest commandment? Who was Judas Iscariot's father? Why was John on the Island of Patmos?

How'd you do on these questions? Which group of questions was easier for you? If you were called to be an expert witness at a trial, what would be the subject on which you would speak? In our work, we gain expertise through training and experience. We know what we do, how to do it, and why it needs to be done. In our hobbies, we submerge ourselves in minor details to increase our understanding. Can we say the same things about our Christian life? After all, is the Christian life not our higher calling? Can we call ourselves expert witnesses on the gospel of Christ? Are you receiving all the power Jesus makes available to you?

In Ephesians 1, Paul explains the power we have through Jesus. He asks for wisdom and revelation for his readers, including us 2,000 years later. He asks us to open our hearts to the power of Jesus and hope for tomorrow. What is that power? It's a power that can calm the winds, resist the devil, and push him away. It's a power that produces much fruit. And the power comes from faith in the one who offers his own power—Jesus Christ. Faith comes from what we hear from the Word. As Christians, we should have a confidence in what we believe. Schedule time every day to read, study, and meditate on God's Word, for it is through hearing the Word that we grow in knowledge, faith, power, and hope for our current circumstances in order to push the devil away and bear fruit.

---❖---

AREN'T YOU PROUD
YOU'RE NOT PROUD?

Moreover Yahweh's word came to me, saying, "Son of man, take up a lamentation over the king of Tyre, and tell him, 'The Lord Yahweh says:

> *"You were the seal of full measure,*
>   *full of wisdom,*
>   *and perfect in beauty.*
> *You were in Eden,*
>   *the garden of God.*
> *Every precious stone adorned you:*
>   *ruby, topaz, emerald,*
>   *chrysolite, onyx, jasper,*
>   *sapphire, turquoise, and beryl.*
> *Gold work of tambourines*
>   *and of pipes was in you.*
>   *They were prepared in the day that you were created.*
> *You were the anointed cherub who covers.*
>   *Then I set you up on the holy mountain of God.*
>   *You have walked up and down in the middle of the stones of fire.*
> *You were perfect in your ways from the day that you were created,*
>   *until unrighteousness was found in you.*
> *By the abundance of your commerce, your insides were filled*
> *with violence,*
>   *and you have sinned.*

Therefore I have cast you as profane out of God's mountain.
  I have destroyed you, covering cherub,
  from the middle of the stones of fire.
Your heart was lifted up because of your beauty.
  You have corrupted your wisdom by reason of your splendor.
I have cast you to the ground.
  I have laid you before kings,
  that they may see you.
By the multitude of your iniquities,
  in the unrighteousness of your commerce,
  you have profaned your sanctuaries.
Therefore I have brought out a fire from the middle of you.
  It has devoured you.
I have turned you to ashes on the earth
  in the sight of all those who see you.
All those who know you among the peoples will be astonished
at you.
  You have become a terror,
  and you will exist no more.'"
                                                    —Ezek. 28:11–19

Now the serpent was more subtle than any animal of the field which Yahweh God had made. He said to the woman, "Has God really said, 'You shall not eat of any tree of the garden'?"

The woman said to the serpent, "We may eat fruit from the trees of the garden, but not the fruit of the tree which is in the middle of the garden. God has said, 'You shall not eat of it. You shall not touch it, lest you die.'"

The serpent said to the woman, "You won't really die, for God knows that in the day you eat it, your eyes will be opened, and you will be like God, knowing good and evil."

When the woman saw that the tree was good for food, and that it was a delight to the eyes, and that the tree was to be desired to make one wise, she took some of its fruit, and ate. Then she gave some to her husband with her, and he ate it, too.

—Gen. 3:1–6

But let each man examine his own work, and then he will have reason to boast in himself, and not in someone else.

—Gal. 6:4

Doing nothing through rivalry or through conceit, but in humility, each counting others better than himself.

—Phil. 2:3

Pride goes before destruction, and an arrogant spirit before a fall.

—Prov. 16:18

When pride comes, then comes shame, but with humility comes wisdom.

—Prov. 11:2

For I say through the grace that was given me, to every man who is among you, not to think of himself more highly than he ought to think; but to think reasonably, as God has apportioned to each person a measure of faith.

—Rom. 12:3

He also spoke this parable to certain people who were convinced of their own righteousness, and who despised all others. "Two men went up into the temple to pray; one was a Pharisee, and the other was a tax collector. The Pharisee stood and prayed to himself like this: 'God, I thank you that I am not like the rest of men, extortionists, unrighteous, adulterers, or even like this tax collector. I fast twice a week. I give tithes of all that I get.' But the tax collector, standing far away, wouldn't even lift up his eyes to heaven, but beat his breast, saying, 'God, be merciful to me, a sinner!' I tell you, this man went down to his house justified rather than the other; for everyone who exalts himself will be humbled, but he who humbles himself will be exalted."

—Luke 18:9–14

He said to them, "What do you want me to do for you?"
They said to him, "Grant to us that we may sit, one at your right hand, and one at your left hand, in your glory."

—Mark 10:36–37

But if anyone thinks that he knows anything, he doesn't yet know as he ought to know.

—1 Cor. 8:2

Humble yourselves in the sight of the Lord, and he will exalt you.

—James 4:10

For it isn't he who commends himself who is approved, but whom the Lord commends.

—2 Cor. 10:18

Have this in your mind, which was also in Christ Jesus, who, existing in the form of God, didn't consider equality with God a thing to be grasped, but emptied himself, taking the form of a servant, being made in the likeness of men. And being found in human form, he humbled himself, becoming obedient to the point of death, yes, the death of the cross. Therefore God also highly exalted him, and gave to him the name which is above every name, that at the name of Jesus every knee should bow,

LETTING GOD'S WORD SPEAK

of those in heaven, those on earth, and those under the earth, and that every tongue should confess that Jesus Christ is Lord, to the glory of God the Father.

—Phil. 2:5–11

Don't be conformed to this world, but be transformed by the renewing of your mind, so that you may prove what is the good, well-pleasing, and perfect will of God.

—Rom. 12:2

Rightly or wrongly, I can tie pride to just about any situation. In Ezekiel, the King of Tyre represents Satan (or Lucifer) in his fall from heaven. Lucifer had it all, including admittance to the Garden of Eden. But he was cast out because of pride. Disguised as a serpent, Satan tempted Eve in the garden. He said she could be like God. While being godly sounds like a noble aspiration, Eve's interest stemmed from her pride.

Lexico defines pride as "a feeling or deep pleasure or satisfaction derived from one's own achievements, the achievements of those with whom one is closely associated, or from qualities or possessions that are widely admired." The problem with pride is usually the attitude that accompanies pride. Galatians indicates that we can be proud of our work. On the other hand, Philippians 2 tells us to do nothing from selfish ambition but rather humbly put others above ourselves. We can be proud of our work, but we must always esteem others above ourselves.

Our pride can cause us problems, as noted in Proverbs. Romans tells us to not think more highly of ourselves than we ought as the Pharisee did in Luke 18 and as James and John showed in Mark 10. The context for us is a bit different, but I think 1 Corinthians makes a strong point that though we may think ourselves wise and knowledgeable, sometimes we just don't know what we're talking about and continue to speak, trusting in our own minds.

I find myself convicted of pride in this very endeavor. I started this journey at God's leading. I had no intention to participate in Facebook and certainly no ambition to write a book, but as I said in the introduction, I clearly heard God's voice say, "Do this for me." I have obeyed. Subjects come to me at various moments. In any one moment, the topic is clearly spoken to me. The direction of the writing is impromptu. Very seldom do I have any phrases in my mind when I begin to write. I study some scriptures based on the topic, choose those that speak to me, and begin. I have no selfish ambition, but there is a fine line between a God-inspired pride and a pride in one's own handiwork. That fine line creeps up on a person, and it is often hard to notice when it's approaching. We need to remember the truth that eluded Eve, the Pharisee, and James and John—it isn't about us.

But there is an antidote for all of us. Jesus offers us grace. James explains that if we humble ourselves—that is, allow him to be our Lord, submit to his ways, and study and follow his Word—he will exalt us. It is not those who commend themselves who are approved but those whom the Lord commends. In Philippians 2, Paul describes how Jesus humbled himself. He came to earth with all the frailties of a human, lived the life of a servant, and died an unbearable death on a cross so that every knee would bow and every tongue confess that He is Lord *"to the glory of the Father."* The key to overcoming pride is doing all to the glory of the Father. We do so by renewing our minds, practicing discernment, and doing what is perfect and acceptable to him.

———— ❖ ————

THE POWER
IN US

Jesus came to them and spoke to them, saying, "All authority has been given to me in heaven and on earth."

—Matt. 28:18

Now to him who is able to do exceedingly abundantly above all that we ask or think, according to the power that works in us, to him be the glory in the assembly and in Christ Jesus to all generations forever and ever. Amen.

—Eph. 3:20–21

If Christ is in you, the body is dead because of sin, but the spirit is alive because of righteousness. But if the Spirit of him who raised up Jesus from the dead dwells in you, he who raised up Christ Jesus from the dead will also give life to your mortal bodies through his Spirit who dwells in you. So then, brothers, we are debtors, not to the flesh, to live after the flesh. For if you live after the flesh, you must die; but if by the Spirit you put to death the deeds of the body, you will live. For as many as are led by the Spirit of God, these are children of God.

Rom. 8:10–14

But Peter said, "I have no silver or gold, but what I have, that I give you. In the name of Jesus Christ of Nazareth, get up and walk!"

—Acts 3:6

Consider this collection of verses concerning the authority and power of the believer. I want to focus on the phrase "the power that works in us," but I think the collection ties together in a progressive message. Before Jesus sent his followers out to make disciples of the world, he reminded them that all authority in heaven and on earth had been given to him. That same authority, Ephesians explains, is power to accomplish far more than we can ask or think. If Christ is in us (notice the word *if*—if you have accepted Jesus as Lord and Savior, he is in you), the *"Spirit [and authority] of him who raised up Jesus from the dead dwells in you."* In Acts, Peter used that same authority to heal the lifelong lameness of the man near the Gate Beautiful. The pattern is established.

Why then do so many Christians accept a life that is less than *"all that we ask or think"*? The answer lies in the phrase *"the power that works in us."* That power has a limiting factor. Whatever power we have at work within us is the maximum God can accomplish. Jesus came on the earth 2,000 years ago and loosed all the power available to him, as noted in the verses above. Hebrews 13:8 tells us that Jesus is the same yesterday, today, and forever. Connecting the dots, that means the power and authority available to Peter are still available to us today. In other words, God, through Jesus, has not changed. That leaves us as the variable part of the equation. The power in each of us is equal (notice that the scripture says *the* power, implying that there is only one level, one power), but "that works" seems to be up to us and varies among us.

Because God works through people, we must listen for and to God's voice. Have you ever considered that you might be the answer to someone else's prayer? What does that mean for them if you aren't listening? Where do we hear God's voice? We hear it in prayer and worship, in study, and in the words of those around us.

God wants a relationship with us. He wants us to spend time with him—in prayer, study, praise, communion, or some other form of relationship. For many, communion (breaking of bread, drinking of wine) is a powerful way to open your heart and mind to his voice through the celebration of his sacrifice. Many people hear God's voice in the still moment of prayer. I hear God's voice most often when I'm studying, reading, or listening to someone else talk about scripture. In fact, most of these topics have come to me in that form—a phrase that I read or heard in a new way.

What do you do to limit God's power within you? Are you spending enough time listening to God? Are you celebrating, taking communion regularly, and not just stepping through the process? Do you have a daily habit of reading and studying scripture? Turn up *"the power that works in"* you. We can claim more power, or we can limit what God can do in us and through us.

❖

COME OUT!

Now a certain man was sick, Lazarus from Bethany, of the village of Mary and her sister, Martha. It was that Mary who had anointed the Lord with ointment and wiped his feet with her hair, whose brother, Lazarus, was sick. The sisters therefore sent to him, saying, "Lord, behold, he for whom you have great affection is sick." But when Jesus heard it, he said, "This sickness is not to death, but for the glory of God, that God's Son may be glorified by it." Now Jesus loved Martha, and her sister, and Lazarus. When therefore he heard that he was sick, he stayed two days in the place where he was. Then after this he said to the disciples, "Let's go into Judea again."

The disciples asked him, "Rabbi, the Jews were just trying to stone you. Are you going there again?"

Jesus answered, "Aren't there twelve hours of daylight? If a man walks in the day, he doesn't stumble, because he sees the light of this world. But if a man walks in the night, he stumbles, because the light isn't in him." He said these things, and after that, he said to them, "Our friend, Lazarus, has fallen asleep, but I am going so that I may awake him out of sleep."

The disciples therefore said, "Lord, if he has fallen asleep, he will recover."

Now Jesus had spoken of his death, but they thought that he spoke of taking rest in sleep. So Jesus said to them plainly *then, "Lazarus is dead. I am glad for your sakes that I was not there, so that you may believe. Nevertheless, let's go to him."*

Thomas therefore, who is called Didymus, said to his fellow disciples, "Let's go also, that we may die with him."

So when Jesus came, he found that he had been in the tomb four days already. Now Bethany was near Jerusalem, about fifteen stadia away. Many of the Jews had joined the women around Martha and Mary, to console them concerning their brother. Then when Martha heard that Jesus was coming, she went and met him, but Mary stayed in the house. Therefore Martha said to Jesus, "Lord, if you would have been here, my brother wouldn't have died. Even now I know that whatever you ask of God, God will give you." Jesus said to her, "Your brother will rise again."

Martha said to him, "I know that he will rise again in the resurrection at the last day."

Jesus said to her, "I am the resurrection and the life. He who believes in me will still live, even if he dies. Whoever lives and believes in me will never die. Do you believe this?"

She said to him, "Yes, Lord. I have come to believe that you are the Christ, God's Son, he who comes into the world."

When she had said this, she went away and called Mary, her sister, secretly, saying, "The Teacher is here and is calling you."

When she heard this, she arose quickly and went to him. Now Jesus had not yet come into the village, but was in the place where Martha met him. Then the Jews who were with her in the house and were consoling her, when they saw Mary, that she rose up quickly and went out, followed her, saying, "She is going to the tomb to weep there." Therefore when Mary came to where Jesus was and saw him, she fell down at his feet, saying to him, "Lord, if you would have been here, my brother wouldn't have died."

When Jesus therefore saw her weeping, and the Jews weeping who came with her, he groaned in the spirit, and was troubled, and said, "Where have you laid him?"

They told him, "Lord, come and see."

Jesus wept.

The Jews therefore said, "See how much affection he had for him!" Some of them said, "Couldn't this man, who opened the eyes of him who was blind, have also kept this man from dying?"

Jesus therefore, again groaning in himself, came to the tomb. Now it was a cave, and a stone lay against it. Jesus said, "Take away the stone."

Martha, the sister of him who was dead, said to him, "Lord, by this time there is a stench, for he has been dead four days."

Jesus said to her, "Didn't I tell you that if you believed, you would see God's glory?"

So they took away the stone from the place where the dead man was lying. Jesus lifted up his eyes, and said, "Father, I thank you that you listened to me. I know that you always listen to me, but because of the multitude standing around I said this, that they may believe that you sent me." When he had said this, he cried with a loud voice, "Lazarus, come out!"

He who was dead came out, bound hand and foot with wrappings, and his face was wrapped around with a cloth.

Jesus said to them, "Free him, and let him go."

—John 11:1–44

When someone you are close to is in crisis, a million emotions run through your mind. Many people today are amazed at Jesus's response to Mary and Martha's urgent message that Lazarus was sick. He delayed for two days. Like Mary and Martha, we often get caught in the immediacy of an issue and forget that *"this sickness is not to death."* Surely God's promise to us through Jesus is stronger than what we are going through at any given moment, but do we see that promise? Are we rooted in the Word enough to remember, or are we consumed with the here and now? Both Mary and Martha knew that Jesus could have saved Lazarus from dying had he been there. Can you imagine their disappointment when Jesus wasn't there when they needed him most, even after they tried to reach him? How often do we think that Jesus was absent when we needed him? How could he let us suffer through this situation by ourselves?

The lesson is that Jesus's perspective is always better than ours, though we often don't see it. We seek our answer in our time. Jesus, in his perfect timing, revealed God's glory. Jesus wasn't physically present when Lazarus died, but he was clearly fully aware of the circumstances. It is no different today. Jesus is fully aware of our circumstances, not the creator of our circumstances. The Bible says that Lazarus was ill, not that Lazarus was being punished by God for sin. When Jesus arrived, Lazarus had been dead for four days. Jesus was emotionally moved by what he saw. *"Jesus wept."* How incredible! When we feel as if Jesus is absent, is it safe to assume that he is moved by our situation and is responding with tears? Lazarus's mourners said, *"See how much affection he had for him!"* Jesus is the same yesterday, today, and tomorrow. He loves us, and he weeps at our pain.

But that is not all he does. Jesus went to Lazarus, even in the tomb—stinking. How bad do our problems stink? Have we let them lie around and rot? Remember, Jesus did not physically arrive on the scene for four days. However, his timing was God's timing and, as always, perfect. Then Jesus called to Lazarus, *"Come out!"*

Jesus is calling us by name today. In the midst of our brokenness, he calls, *"Come out!"* In the midst of our selfishness, he calls, *"Come out!"* In the midst of our grief, he calls, *"Come out!"* In the midst of our pride, he calls, *"Come out!"* No matter our situation, Jesus knows our name, weeps at our pain, and then confidently calls us to *"Come out!"* And we, like Lazarus, must hear his voice, leave ourselves behind, and respond.

THE BEST
IS YET TO COME

*The third day, there was a wedding in Cana of Galilee. Jesus'
mother was there. Jesus also was invited, with his disciples,
to the wedding. When the wine ran out, Jesus' mother said to
him, "They have no wine."*

*Jesus said to her, "Woman, what does that have to do
with you and me? My hour has not yet come."*

*His mother said to the servants, "Whatever he says to
you, do it." Now there were six water pots of stone set there
after the Jews' way of purifying, containing two or three
metretes apiece. Jesus said to them, "Fill the water pots
with water." So they filled them up to the brim. He said to
them, "Now draw some out, and take it to the ruler of the
feast." So they took it. When the ruler of the feast tasted the
water now become wine, and didn't know where it came
from (but the servants who had drawn the water knew), the
ruler of the feast called the bridegroom and said to him,
"Everyone serves the good wine first, and when the guests
have drunk freely, then that which is worse. You have kept
the good wine until now!" This beginning of his signs Jesus
did in Cana of Galilee, and revealed his glory; and his
disciples believed in him.*

—John 2:1–11

The thief only comes to steal, kill, and destroy. I came that they may have life, and may have it abundantly.

—John 10:10

May mercy, peace, and love be multiplied to you.

—Jude 2

And God is able to make all grace abound to you, that you, always having all sufficiency in everything, may abound to every good work.

—2 Cor. 9:8

Blessed be the God and Father of our Lord Jesus Christ, who according to his great mercy caused us to be born again to a living hope through the resurrection of Jesus Christ from the dead, to an incorruptible and undefiled inheritance that doesn't fade away, reserved in Heaven for you, who by the power of God are guarded through faith for a salvation ready to be revealed in the last time.

—1 Pet. 1:3–5

For our light affliction, which is for the moment, works for us more and more exceedingly an eternal weight of glory, while we don't look at the things which are seen, but at the things which are not seen. For the things which are seen are temporal, but the things which are not seen are eternal.

—2 Cor. 4:17–18

For we don't have here an enduring city, but we seek that which is to come.

—Heb. 13:14

The construction of its wall was jasper. The city was pure gold, like pure glass. The foundations of the city's wall were adorned with all kinds of precious stones. The first foundation was jasper; the second, sapphire; the third, chalcedony; the fourth, emerald; the fifth, sardonyx; the sixth, sardius; the seventh, chrysolite; the eighth, beryl; the ninth, topaz; the tenth, chrysoprase; the eleventh, jacinth; and the twelfth, amethyst. The twelve gates were twelve pearls. Each one of the gates was made of one pearl. The street of the city was pure gold, like transparent glass. I saw no temple in it, for the Lord God, the Almighty, and the Lamb, are its temple. The city has no need for the sun or moon to shine, for the very glory of God illuminated it, and its lamp is the Lamb. The nations will walk in its light. The kings of the earth bring the glory and honor of the nations into it.

—Rev. 21:18–24

He showed me a river of water of life, clear as crystal, proceeding out of the throne of God and of the Lamb, in the middle of its street. On this side of the river and on that was the tree of life, bearing twelve kinds of fruits, yielding its fruit every month. The leaves of the tree were for the healing of the nations. There will be no curse any more. The throne of God and of the Lamb will be in it, and his servants will serve him. They will see his face, and his name will be on their foreheads. There will be no night, and they need no lamp light or sun light; for the Lord God will illuminate them. They will reign forever and ever.

—Rev. 22:1–5

I have always respected Jesus's first miracle (or "sign," as John called it), for it revealed Jesus's character. It showed his love for his mother, his compassion for the family at the wedding, and his authority over the world. But for me, it didn't have the deeper meaning the other signs did. Then one Sunday, the Holy Spirit revealed to me two new concepts about the wedding at Cana.

The first is the concept of abundance. Jesus didn't just change a little water into wine; he changed 120–150 gallons of water into wine! We should expect abundance when Jesus works in our lives. Jesus said he came to give life abundantly. But it isn't just that we may live in abundance; it's that by having enough, we share our abundance with others. At Cana, Jesus shared his abundance with the family at the wedding, and they shared their abundance with their guests.

The second concept is that the best is yet to come. Traditionally, the best wine was served first. Once the guests were a bit less "distinguishing," the wine quality was lessened, assuming the guests wouldn't notice. But Jesus saved the best wine (or created the best wine) for last. Similarly, we assume first is best. We try to be first in line to get what we can get from this life; but our real life, our *best* life, is yet to come. Fame, fortune, and status are temporary; they will all fade away. How many people do you know who have let the days of this life consume them? The troubles of today—finances, employment, family, health—are not (or should not be) our long-term focus.

Albert Brumley wrote the great hymn "This World Is Not My Home." That should be our attitude. We're only passing through here. Our best life is stored up for us in heaven. Paul tells us to look upon the unseen, the eternal. The writer of Hebrews reminds us that we have no city here; look for what is to come. Finally, John, as shown to him in Revelation, gives us a glimpse of the new earth, a city so rich that it has giant pearls for gates and streets of gold so pure they're transparent. Things this world finds precious are used simply as building materials. John tells of a place where the Tree of Life bears its fruit, a new fruit each month, and the Lamb is the light. How incredible!

Don't let yourself get comfortable in this life or fret about the complications we all face. Jesus brought the best wine to the wedding feast later. God, through Jesus and with the Holy Spirit inside us, is calling us to a better life today and a best life in heaven. He has prepared a spectacular place for us. The best is truly yet to come!

---❖---

OMNI

In the beginning, God created the heavens and the earth. The earth was formless and empty. Darkness was on the surface of the deep and God's Spirit was hovering over the surface of the waters. God said, "Let there be light," and there was light.

—Gen. 1:1–3

He counts the number of the stars.
  He calls them all by their names.
Great is our Lord, and mighty in power.
  His understanding is infinite.

—Ps. 147:4–5

Where could I go from your Spirit?
  Or where could I flee from your presence?

—Ps. 139:7

I command you before God, who gives life to all things, and before Christ Jesus, who before Pontius Pilate testified the good confession, that you keep the commandment without spot, blameless, until the appearing of our Lord Jesus Christ, which in its own times he will show, who is the blessed and only Ruler, the King of kings, and Lord of lords.

—1 Tim. 6:13–15

They heard Yahweh God's voice walking in the garden in the cool of the day, and the man and his wife hid themselves from the presence of Yahweh God among the trees of the garden.

—Gen. 3:8

But Jonah rose up to flee to Tarshish from the presence of Yahweh. He went down to Joppa, and found a ship going to Tarshish; so he paid its fare, and went down into it, to go with them to Tarshish from the presence of Yahweh.

—Jon. 1:3

Because they have forsaken me, and have defiled this place, and have burned incense in it to other gods that they didn't know, they, their fathers, and the kings of Judah, and have filled this place with the blood of innocents, and have built the high places of Baal, to burn their children in the fire for burnt offerings to Baal, which I didn't command, nor speak, which didn't even enter into my mind.

—Jer. 19:4–5

Let's come before his presence with thanksgiving.
Let's extol him with songs!

—Ps. 95:2

In 1978, Chrysler Corporation introduced two new models to their lineup: the Plymouth Horizon and the Dodge Omni. We had a 1978 Omni that stayed with us for several years. In fact, I'm quite sure that was the car I drove to take my driver's license test. The advertising tagline for the car was an obvious play on the meaning of the Latin word *omni*—"all."

We use the same Latin word *omni* as a prefix to describe God: all-powerful (omnipotent), all-knowing (omniscient), and all-present (omnipresent). Certainly, the creation story proves God is all-powerful. After all, he created everything from nothing. Can you get more powerful than that? Likewise, God omnisciently understands his vast creation. He numbered and then named all the stars. David could find no place where God's omnipresent Spirit did not reside. God is sovereign. In fact, Timothy calls Jesus Sovereign, *"King of kings, and Lord of lords."* But is God always omni? Or do we have a role?

Most Christians define our sovereign God as a ruler of the universe doing whatever he wants and completely controlling everything. Let me make some counterarguments. I believe we can rely too much on the "allness" of God, and we use the sovereignty of God as an excuse for many things. I will not argue God's omnipresence. However, I will argue that we can be out of his presence. After Adam and Eve ate the forbidden fruit, they specifically hid themselves from God's presence. When God told Jonah to go to Nineveh and speak against the wickedness in the city, Jonah fled from the presence of God. What is the common denominator? They turned against the will of God. While God is always present and we can't hide from him, we clearly can move away from him. As they say, when you no longer feel close to God, it isn't God who has moved.

Likewise, God is omniscient. However, three times in Jeremiah, he described the people of Judah sacrificing their children to the idols of Baal (Jer. 7:31–32, 19:4–5, 32:35). God was clearly angry with their action, so angry that he ultimately sent them into exile in Babylon. But notice the line, *"which didn't even enter into my mind."* It appears that we not only can leave God's presence, but we can also do things so abominable that he hasn't even imagined our deeds. Our all-knowing God does not think as we do. Yes, he knew they had done these things, as he knows when we stray, but he didn't imagine it before they did it.

Do you think God controls every movement of every person or every circumstance that happens? I don't see those as descriptors of a loving God. Since we know God is everywhere, knows everything, and can do anything, we often assume that we have no role in our own lives—that God truly is in full control. But that idea doesn't square with the Word. Yes, God set rules in place that the universe must follow. The earth will rotate around the sun based on his path and pace. Gravity does not randomly suspend itself. Electricity always reacts the same way. Water never runs uphill. God set rules in place to keep the universe stable. From that perspective, he is all-powerful. But I would be extremely disappointed if God *caused* the mistakes I make, that he *causes* me to say unkind things in the heat of the moment (or in the tired part of the day), that he *causes* racial or political violence, that he *causes* bad things to happen to good people.

I think we should consider the meaning of the word *sovereign*— "having supreme rank, power, or authority; Supreme; Preeminent; Indisputable; Greatest in degree; Utmost or extreme; Being above all others in character, importance, excellence, etc."[1] Of course, our sovereign God should be our Lord. He should be the highest authority, preeminent. But we have to allow him that role in our lives; he won't just take it.

There is a path to God. In Psalm 95, God invites us back into his presence and asks us to come with thanksgiving. Yes, he has plans for us, but it is completely up to us to accept his plans, including the plan to save us for eternity through Jesus. But we have to seek, we have to ask, and we have to find. We have to make him supreme. We have to make him our indisputable Lord. Consider these additional scriptures:

> *"For I know the thoughts that I think toward you," says Yahweh, "thoughts of peace, and not of evil, to give you hope and a future. You shall call on me, and you shall go and pray to me, and I will listen to you. You shall seek me, and find me, when you search for me with all your heart."*
>
> —Jer. 29:11–13

> *For God so loved the world, that he gave his one and only Son, that whoever believes in him should not perish, but have eternal life. For God didn't send his Son into the world to judge the world, but that the world should be saved through him.*
>
> —John 3:16–17

---

1. *Random House Kernerman Webster's College Dictionary* (2010), s.v. "sovereign."

Ask, and it will be given you. Seek, and you will find.
Knock, and it will be opened for you. For everyone who asks
receives. He who seeks finds. To him who knocks it will be
opened.

—Matt. 7:7–8

Finally, brothers, whatever things are true, whatever things
are honorable, whatever things are just, whatever things are
pure, whatever things are lovely, whatever things are of good
report: if there is any virtue and if there is any praise, think
about these things.

—Phil. 4:8

We must seek him. If we do, we will find him. We must believe him.
If we do, we will have eternal life. We must elevate him to first place in
our lives!

What then shall we say about these things? If God is for us,
who can be against us?

—Rom. 8:31

---❖---

LUCKENBACH,
TEXAS

For God so loved the world, that he gave his one and only Son, that whoever believes in him should not perish, but have eternal life.

—John 3:16

Jesus said to him, "I am the way, the truth, and the life. No one comes to the Father, except through me. If you had known me, you would have known my Father also. From now on, you know him, and have seen him."

—John 14:6–7

By this we know that we remain in him and he in us, because he has given us of his Spirit.

—1 John 4:13

Jesus came to them and spoke to them, saying, "All authority has been given to me in heaven and on earth. Go and make disciples of all nations, baptizing them in the name of the Father and of the Son and of the Holy Spirit, teaching them to observe all things that I commanded you. Behold, I am with you always, even to the end of the age." Amen.

—Matt. 28:18–20

I've spent some time researching statistics about Christians in the United States and in the world. According to the Pew Research Center, the number of American adults describing themselves as Christians (including Catholics) is currently 65 percent, down 12 percent in the last decade. At the same time, 26 percent identify as "none," claiming no religious affiliation, up an astounding 17 percent in the last decade. "Nones" are people who claim no affiliation with religion, not people who merely claim no denomination. More adults in the United States now say they attend a religious service (excluding weddings and funerals) only occasionally or not at all than those who say they attend at least once or twice a month.

The decline is strictly generational. Those born between 1928 and 1964 are as likely to identify as Christians as they were a decade ago. But in the millennial and younger generations, less than half identify as Christian, and only about 36 percent attend a religious service regularly (once or twice a month). The decline in church attendance refers to how many people are attending, not to how often people attend. The number of those identifying as Christian has dropped from 178 million 10 years ago to 167 million now. Nones have increased by more than 30 million in that same time frame.

A decade ago, 57 percent of Hispanics described themselves as Catholic. That number is now 47 percent. The nones within the Hispanic population are now 23 percent. From a gender perspective, men are more likely to describe themselves as nones, at 30 percent, compared to 23 percent of women, who are also more likely to attend a religious service regularly than men. Those attendance numbers have dropped to 50 percent for women and 40 percent for men.

When you look at the Pew Research Center information from a global perspective, you see a bit different picture. The number of identifying Christians in the world today stands at an estimated 2.3 billion, making Christianity the largest religion (*relationship* is a better word, in my opinion) on the planet. This is up from 2.2 billion just 10 years ago, representing 32 percent of the world's population. Nones represent about

16 percent of the world's population and are the third-largest group. Christianity is growing the fastest in Africa and China.[2]

So where does that leave us, and why the strange title for this chapter? Let's address the title first. For those of you who know the Waylon Jennings and Willie Nelson song "Luckenbach, Texas," you know the premise of the song is that life can get too complicated and that sometimes we just need to go back to where it all started. Maybe it's time those of us who identify ourselves as Christians get back to the church's beginnings as well.

Also included in the Pew Research information was this staggering number: 41,000 worldwide Christian denominations. I can think of three basic reasons for groups to form a new church. One, the congregation has outgrown itself and needs more space. That's an explanation for a new place of worship, not a new denomination. Two, worship style. There are denominations (or nondenominations) that set themselves apart over worship. And three, there are differences in beliefs, the most prominent reason for starting a new denomination.

History is full of denominational splits. The Anglican Church split from the Catholic Church. What is now the United Methodist Church is a split from the Anglican Church, and the United Methodist Church is currently suffering the threat of a split. The Christian Church (Disciples of Christ) and the Church of Christ are splits from the Christian Church, which resulted from two movements away from the rigid denominational rules of the Presbyterian and Baptist causes of the early 1800s. And so it goes within numerous denominations, not to mention the proliferation of independent churches that call themselves nondenominational.

Is it possible we've made it too complicated for the next generations or those who are not yet believers? What if for the mathematical equation 2 + 2 there were 41,000 options for an answer? Would anyone figure out how to solve math problems? My question is this: Are there some basic principles upon which we can agree to be Christians and leave the carpet color issues

---

2. "In U.S., Decline of Christianity Continues at Rapid Pace," *Pew Research Center*, October 17, 2019, https://www.pewforum.org/2019/10/17/in-u-s-decline-of-christianity-continues-at-rapid-pace/.

to the side? To me, the essentials are what decisions and beliefs will get you to heaven and what decisions and beliefs will keep you from heaven. Will singing to a musical instrument in church keep you from heaven? Will being baptized by sprinkling and not immersion keep you from heaven? Will taking communion once every three months instead of every day keep you from heaven? Will not reading the Holy Bible every day keep you from heaven?

All these practices may be spiritual disciplines that sharpen our focus on Jesus and draw us closer to God, or they might be preferences that make us feel comfortable, but they are divisions that tend to separate us when we make them essential or dogmatic. Why is it bad for Christians to go their separate ways and disagree about biblical principles? It is because when we are fighting each other or even disagreeing with each other without listening, we're not working to bring others to Christ.

God loved the world enough to send us his Son as a sacrifice and an example. The path to heaven is through Jesus. In John's Gospel, Jesus emphatically states that he is the only way to the Father. Can we agree that Jesus is God's only Son, that through believing in him—his crucifixion and resurrection—we find eternal life with the Father? Agreeing that Jesus is God's Son, we must believe in God as our supreme Father. Believing in the Father and the Son leads us to believe in the Holy Spirit as our comforter and advocate. And to believe in the three, we must trust the Holy Scripture as God's inspired Word. These points should be enough to help us work together rather than pull us in different directions.

There are many points we can disagree on. Two billion people reading the Holy Bible are bound to interpret a verse or two differently. It's more important to find the points we do agree on. We shouldn't let points of disagreement or even different understandings be points of division. Each of us is responsible to study the scriptures for ourselves and learn what they say to us. Sure, it's great to share our thoughts with others. It's great to hear what others think and evaluate and compare them with our own beliefs. It's fun to learn. But it isn't practical to expect everyone to think exactly as we do, and it isn't practical to expect that you're always right (yes, I've been wrong on occasion).

Maybe it's time we go back to God's love.

I HAVE
TO DO WHAT?

Jude, a servant of Jesus Christ, and brother of James, to those who are called, sanctified by God the Father, and kept for Jesus Christ: May mercy, peace, and love be multiplied to you.

Beloved, while I was very eager to write to you about our common salvation, I was constrained to write to you exhorting you to contend earnestly for the faith which was once for all delivered to the saints. For there are certain men who crept in secretly, even those who were long ago written about for this condemnation: ungodly men, turning the grace of our God into indecency, and denying our only Master, God, and Lord, Jesus Christ.

Now I desire to remind you, though you already know this, that the Lord, having saved a people out of the land of Egypt, afterward destroyed those who didn't believe. Angels who didn't keep their first domain, but deserted their own dwelling place, he has kept in everlasting bonds under darkness for the judgment of the great day. Even as Sodom and Gomorrah and the cities around them, having in the same way as these given themselves over to sexual immorality and gone after strange flesh, are shown as an example, suffering the punishment of eternal fire. Yet in the same way, these also in their dreaming defile the flesh, despise authority, and slander celestial beings. But Michael, the archangel, when contending with the devil and arguing about the body of Moses, dared not bring against him an abusive condemnation, but said, "May the Lord rebuke you!" But these speak evil of whatever things they don't know. They are destroyed in these things that they understand naturally, like the creatures without reason. Woe to them! For they went in the way of Cain, and ran riotously in the error of Balaam for hire, and perished in Korah's rebellion. These are hidden rocky reefs in your love feasts when they feast with you, shepherds who without fear feed themselves; clouds without water, carried along by winds; autumn trees without fruit, twice dead, plucked up by the roots; wild waves of the sea, foaming out their own shame; wandering stars, for whom the blackness of darkness has been reserved forever. About these also Enoch, the seventh from Adam, prophesied, saying, "Behold, the Lord came with ten thousands of his holy ones, to execute judgment on all, and to convict all the ungodly of all their works of ungodliness which they have done in an ungodly way, and of all the hard things which ungodly sinners have spoken against him." These are murmurers and complainers, walking after their lusts—and their mouth speaks proud things—showing respect of persons to gain advantage.

But you, beloved, keep building up yourselves on your most holy faith, praying in the Holy Spirit. Keep yourselves in God's love, looking for the mercy of our Lord Jesus Christ to eternal life. On some have compassion, making a distinction, and some save, snatching them out of the fire with fear, hating even the clothing stained by the flesh.

Now to him who is able to keep them from stumbling, and to present you faultless before the presence of his glory in great joy, to God our Savior, who alone is wise, be glory and majesty, dominion and power, both now and forever. Amen.

—Jude 1–25

Now very early in the morning, he came again into the temple, and all the people came to him. He sat down and taught them. The scribes and the Pharisees brought a woman taken in adultery. Having set her in the middle, they told him, "Teacher, we found this woman in adultery, in the very act. Now in our law, Moses commanded us to stone such women. What then do you say about her?" They said this testing him, that they might have something to accuse him of.

But Jesus stooped down and wrote on the ground with his finger. But when they continued asking him, he looked up and said to them, "He who is without sin among you, let him throw the first stone at her." Again he stooped down and wrote on the ground with his finger.

They, when they heard it, being convicted by their conscience, went out one by one, beginning from the oldest, even to the last. Jesus was left alone with the woman where she was, in the middle. Jesus, standing up, saw her and said, "Woman, where are your accusers? Did no one condemn you?"

She said, "No one, Lord."

Jesus said, "Neither do I condemn you. Go your way. From now on, sin no more."

—John 8:2–11

Now in Jerusalem by the sheep gate, there is a pool, which is called in Hebrew, "Bethesda," having five porches. In these lay a great multitude of those who were sick, blind, lame, or paralyzed, waiting for the moving of the water; for an angel went down at certain times into the pool and stirred up the water. Whoever stepped in first after the stirring of the water was healed of whatever disease he had. A certain man was there who had been sick for thirty-eight years. When Jesus saw him lying there, and knew that he had been sick for a long time, he asked him, "Do you want to be made well?"

The sick man answered him, "Sir, I have no one to put me into the pool when the water is stirred up, but while I'm coming, another steps down before me."

Jesus said to him, "Arise, take up your mat, and walk."

Immediately, the man was made well, and took up his mat and walked.

Now it was the Sabbath on that day. So the Jews said to him who was cured, "It is the Sabbath. It is not lawful for you to carry the mat."

He answered them, "He who made me well said to me, 'Take up your mat and walk.'"

Then they asked him, "Who is the man who said to you, 'Take up your mat and walk'?"

But he who was healed didn't know who it was, for Jesus had withdrawn, a crowd being in the place.

Afterward Jesus found him in the temple, and said to him, "Behold, you are made well. Sin no more, so that nothing worse happens to you."

—John 5:2–14

From that time, Jesus began to preach, and to say, "Repent! For the Kingdom of Heaven is at hand."

—Matt. 4:17

The early Christians were threatened for their beliefs. The formerly established religious leaders were afraid of losing their authority and status. The government feared Christianity would turn into some political threat to their power and authority. But the biggest threat to Christianity was within its own gates: false doctrine (information). The letter from Jude (a son of Mary and Joseph) to an unknown recipient warns readers to *"contend earnestly for the faith"* by rejecting false teachings, remembering God's salvation and also his punishment, and to *"keep building up yourselves on your most holy faith."* Let's talk about these points in today's context.

Contending for the faith is personal, for each of us needs to develop our own understanding of God's Word and thus our own relationship with God through Jesus. But contending for the faith is also a broader discussion about the unity of the body of Christ, removing those nonessential walls that cause us to waste time fighting instead of working to bring others into the body.

One of the greatest threats to Christianity today is not knowing the scriptures. John 8:31–32 recounts, *"Jesus therefore said to those Jews who had believed him, 'If you remain in my word, then you are truly my disciples. You will know the truth, and the truth will make you free.'"* It is only the truth you know that can make you free. If you don't know the Word, you will not recognize false teaching when it comes your way. The trouble with false teaching is that it can sound like good doctrine. Take, for instance, the broadly popular idea that all you have to do is be nice. There is truth in that phrase, but "all" kills it. Jude brings up several examples of God's forgiveness, but he notes several times that God chastised His people as well. Those examples are Old Testament examples, and we're under a new covenant with Jesus. So what does the New Testament say?

In John 8, Jesus shows compassion to the woman caught in adultery (and let's not forget that this story is as much about his reaction as it is his action). However, his compassion had an expectation: *"From now on, sin no more."* In the story of the man healed at the pool, Jesus specifically asked the man whether he wanted to be healed. Jesus had compassion because of the man's physical ailment, but he also saw inside the man and commanded him to *"sin no more"* (John 5:14). The man's sin didn't cause his lameness, but Jesus's compassion ought to cause a changed heart. Early in Jesus's ministry, he commanded followers to repent. The word *repent* means "change." Jesus expects an action from us.

We as knowing Christians must not be fooled by the all-you-have-to-do-is-be-nice doctrine, and we must not perpetuate that notion to new believers. It doesn't go far enough. It negates the belief in Jesus as the only way to God (John 3:16, John 14) and devalues God's grace. Grace was not a free gift. Jesus paid an unimaginable, incredible price for the grace available to us. He was beaten beyond recognition, and then he hung on a cross, died, and lay in a tomb for three days. Worst of all, he was separated from his Father as he took on our sins—separated so that we might never experience such separation.

What is the meaning of grace if we have no responsibility in the process? Is Jesus worth so little to us that we can continue in our sin? Of course, we won't always get it right, for we live in a fallen world. But imperfection is no excuse not to try our best to follow Jesus and his teachings. Our actions have consequences. I have type 2 diabetes. One explanation is that it runs in my family. Knowing that, how did I respond? I ate chocolate chip cookies, chocolate milk, ice cream, biscuits and gravy, 3 Musketeers candy, peach iced tea, pineapple juice—I wonder if my situation is a consequence of my actions. I fully believe this condition will not get me down, that a period of medication will have my organs and cells functioning once again as designed, but I have to do something else as well. All those foods listed above—they're gone. I can't keep doing what I was doing and expect healing. We can't receive grace and go on as if nothing in our life has changed.

Finally, Jude tells us to build ourselves up and keep ourselves in God's love. How do we accomplish that? Know scripture and communicate with God daily. We have to study scripture, for *"faith comes by hearing, and hearing by the word of God"* (Rom. 10:17). My challenge to you is this: Don't just read. Get a good study aid to help you understand the text, context, history, and connectivity of each verse. No verse in the Holy Bible stands alone; all are critical to the message God has for us. A study aid will help you connect verses to each other and bring the totality of the Bible alive to you. Commune with God each day, and pray. Prayer is more about listening than talking. Ask God to speak to you. He'll find a way if you earnestly desire him (Matt. 7:7). The daily act of communion is a great way to humble yourself before your Savior.

I'll end this with Jude's closing words (verse 25): *"Now to him who is able to keep them from stumbling, and to present you faultless before the presence of his glory in great joy, to God our Savior, who alone is wise, be glory and majesty, dominion and power, both now and forever. Amen."*

---·❖·---

REVELATION
(IN SHORT)

This is the Revelation of Jesus Christ, which God gave him to show to his servants the things which must happen soon, which he sent and made known by his angel to his servant, John, who testified to God's word and of the testimony of Jesus Christ, about everything that he saw.

Blessed is he who reads and those who hear the words of the prophecy, and keep the things that are written in it, for the time is at hand.

—Rev. 1:1–3

I was in the Spirit on the Lord's day, and I heard behind me a loud voice, like a trumpet saying, "What you see, write in a book and send to the seven assemblies: to Ephesus, Smyrna, Pergamum, Thyatira, Sardis, Philadelphia, and to Laodicea."

I turned to see the voice that spoke with me. Having turned, I saw seven golden lamp stands. And among the lamp stands was one like a son of man clothed with a robe reaching down to his feet, and with a golden sash around his chest. His head and his hair were white as white wool, like snow. His eyes were like a flame of fire. His feet were like burnished brass, as if it had been refined in a furnace. His voice was like the voice of many waters. He had seven stars in his right hand. Out of his mouth proceeded a sharp two-edged sword. His face was like the sun shining at its brightest.

—Rev. 1:10–16

I saw in the middle of the throne and of the four living creatures, and in the middle of the elders, a Lamb standing, as though it had been slain, having seven horns and seven eyes, which are the seven Spirits of God, sent out into all the earth. Then he came, and he took it out of the right hand of him who sat on the throne. Now when he had taken the book, the four living creatures and the twenty-four elders fell down before the Lamb, each one having a harp, and golden bowls full of incense, which are the prayers of the saints. They sang a new song, saying,

> *"You are worthy to take the book*
>> *and to open its seals:*
> *for you were killed,*
>> *and bought us for God with your blood*
>> *out of every tribe, language, people, and nation,*
> *and made us kings and priests to our God,*
>> *and we will reign on the earth."*

I saw, and I heard something like a voice of many angels around the throne, the living creatures, and the elders. The number of them was ten thousands of ten thousands, and thousands of thousands; saying with a loud voice, "Worthy is the Lamb who has been killed to receive the power, wealth, wisdom, strength, honor, glory, and blessing!"

I heard every created thing which is in heaven, on the earth, under the earth, on the sea, and everything in them, saying, "To him who sits on the throne, and to the Lamb be the blessing, the honor, the glory, and the dominion, forever and ever! Amen!"

—Rev. 5:6–13

The shapes of the locusts were like horses prepared for war. On their heads were something like golden crowns, and their faces were like people's faces. They had hair like women's hair, and their teeth were like those of lions. They had breastplates, like breastplates of iron. The sound of their wings was like the sound of chariots, or of many horses rushing to war. They have tails like those of scorpions, and stings. In their tails they have power to harm men for five months. They have over them as king the angel of the abyss. His name in Hebrew is "Abaddon," but in Greek, he has the name "Apollyon."

—Rev. 9:7–11

There was war in the sky. Michael and his angels made war on the dragon. The dragon and his angels made war. They didn't prevail. No place was found for them any more in heaven. The great dragon was thrown down, the old serpent, he who is called the devil and Satan, the deceiver of the whole world. He was thrown down to the earth, and his angels were thrown down with him.

—Rev. 12:7–9

Then I stood on the sand of the sea. I saw a beast coming up out of the sea, having ten horns and seven heads. On his horns were ten crowns, and on his heads, blasphemous names. The beast which I saw was like a leopard, and his feet were like those of a bear, and his mouth like the mouth of a lion. The dragon gave him his power, his throne, and great authority. One of his heads looked like it had been wounded fatally. His fatal wound was healed, and the whole earth marveled at the beast. They worshiped the dragon, because he gave his authority to the beast, and they worshiped the beast, saying, "Who is like the beast? Who is able to make war with him?"

—Rev. 13:1–4

I saw the heaven opened, and behold, a white horse, and he who sat on it is called Faithful and True. In righteousness he judges and makes war. His eyes are a flame of fire, and on his head are many crowns. He has names written and a name written which no one knows but he himself. He is clothed in a garment sprinkled with blood. His name is called "The Word of God." The armies which are in heaven followed him on white horses, clothed in white, pure, fine linen. Out of his mouth proceeds a sharp, double-edged sword, that with it he should strike the nations. He will rule them with an iron rod. He treads the wine press of the fierceness of the wrath of God, the Almighty. He has on his garment and on his thigh a name written, "KING OF KINGS, AND LORD OF LORDS."

I saw an angel standing in the sun. He cried with a loud voice, saying to all the birds that fly in the sky, "Come! Be gathered together to the great supper of God, that you may eat the flesh of kings, the flesh of captains, the flesh of mighty men, and the flesh of horses and of those who sit on them, and the flesh of all men, both free and slave, small and great." I saw the beast, and the kings of the earth, and their armies, gathered together to make war against him who sat on the horse, and against his army. The beast was taken, and with him the false prophet who worked the signs in his sight, with which he deceived those who had received the mark of the beast and those who worshiped his image. These two were thrown alive into the lake of fire that burns with sulfur. The rest were killed with the sword of him who sat on the horse, the sword which came out of his mouth. So all the birds were filled with their flesh.

—Rev. 19:11–21

I saw a new heaven and a new earth: for the first heaven and the first earth have passed away, and the sea is no more. I saw the holy city, New Jerusalem, coming down out of heaven from

God, prepared like a bride adorned for her husband. I heard a loud voice out of heaven saying, "Behold, God's dwelling is with people, and he will dwell with them, and they will be his people, and God himself will be with them as their God. He will wipe away every tear from their eyes. Death will be no more; neither will there be mourning, nor crying, nor pain, any more. The first things have passed away."

—Rev. 21:1–4

He showed me a river of water of life, clear as crystal, proceeding out of the throne of God and of the Lamb, in the middle of its street. On this side of the river and on that was the tree of life, bearing twelve kinds of fruits, yielding its fruit every month. The leaves of the tree were for the healing of the nations. There will be no curse any more. The throne of God and of the Lamb will be in it, and his servants will serve him. They will see his face, and his name will be on their foreheads. There will be no night, and they need no lamp light or sun light; for the Lord God will illuminate them. They will reign forever and ever.

—Rev. 22:1–5

"Behold, I come quickly. My reward is with me, to repay to each man according to his work. I am the Alpha and the Omega, the First and the Last, the Beginning and the End. Blessed are those who do his commandments, that they may have the right to the tree of life, and may enter in by the gates into the city. Outside are the dogs, the sorcerers, the sexually immoral, the murderers, the idolaters, and everyone who loves and practices falsehood. I, Jesus, have sent my angel to testify these things to you for the assemblies. I am the root and the offspring of David, the Bright and Morning Star."

—Rev. 22:12–16

I've always enjoyed the book of Revelation. I've read it several times, gone through several studies, and even led a study of it a couple of times. However, I recently read the book, all 22 chapters, in one sitting for the first time. Reading the entire book in one sitting allowed the seeming complexity of the various symbols to fade, and in their place a basic outline of the book shined with what I believe to be the essence of the message. Revelation ends with an admonition to neither add to nor take away from the words of the book. My intention here is to obey that command. Please don't take this overview as a reason to avoid a full study of the book. This is a simple perspective to introduce the book to those who have previously been afraid to read it.

John, the beloved disciple, wrote Revelation near the end of his life as he was exiled for preaching Jesus's gospel. Millions of books have attempted to reveal the deep meanings of the book, people, places, and times. Some believe it was a code for the first century church to keep the faith and not give up hope. Some believe it was written in precise, literal terms to describe a future time when the world as we know it will end. Still others enjoy the mystery of the symbols and try to apply them to specific events in history. I think Revelation is a call to the contemporary church—whether it's the church reading John's writing in the first century, the church of today, or the church 1,000 years from now—to keep the faith, never give up hope, know that God reigns supreme, and understand that we have a role in God's plan.

John describes several scenes. He begins with letters to the seven churches, describes worship of the Holy Father and Son, concedes that Adam and Eve gave Satan dominion over the earth, explains the ultimate struggle between good and evil (Jesus and Satan), and ends with a victory celebration.

In this broad overview, don't get too caught up with the names of the churches, the number of churches, or their locations. Focus on the messages to the churches. You exist to love and proclaim Jesus's grace. You must stand up for the Word. You must worship the true God and never replace him with false gods. You must do the good works for which the church was founded. You must not give up or rely on your own success. These messages still apply to today's church and to individual believers. Our roles in God's greater plan are to proclaim, witness, worship, do, and trust.

John describes the angels and other beings worshiping the Father and the Son in heaven as it has been since the beginning and will always be. God designed all beings to worship him, not because he needs our worship but because we need to worship him. Only the perfect Lamb (Jesus) is worthy to be praised and worthy to take on the sin and corruption of the world as the perfect sacrifice for the judgment of the Father. We find complete joy in worshiping him who created us, saved us, and sustains us.

John then uses several symbols to describe Satan's dominion of the earth. We know that it wasn't God's plan for Satan to have dominion over the earth; mankind handed over the earth's dominion to Satan in Eden. As you recall, God created mankind to rule over all the earth (Gen. 1:25–31). When Adam and Eve ate of the tree of the knowledge of good and evil, God removed them from Eden and cursed mankind to work and be at constant strife with Satan (Gen. 3:13–24). I look at John's symbols of beasts and serpents and plagues and woes as I do at old Westerns. Back in the day, the bad guys wore black cowboy hats, and the good guys wore white cowboy hats. Read Revelation from the perspective that all the various "black hats" represent Satan and his minions, and assume the "white hats" represent Jesus's saving grace.

One other symbol I think important is the symbol of the great city of Babylon. In Jeremiah, Lamentations, and Ezekiel, the city of Babylon represents the worship of idols and other gods. God punished Israel with captivity in Babylon because they turned their backs on him and worshiped other gods. The fall of Babylon correlated with Revelation's description of humans no longer worshiping other gods.

John concludes with a description of the new heaven and the new earth. There are multiple opinions on when this will happen. From my perspective, the important thing is that it *will* happen. When Jesus left the tomb, the battle described in Revelation was won. Revelation 1:17–18 says,

"*When I saw him, I fell at his feet like a dead man. He laid his right hand on me, saying, 'Don't be afraid. I am the first and the last, and the Living one. I was dead, and behold, I am alive forever and ever. Amen. I have the keys of Death and of Hades.'*" Notice that Jesus didn't tell John he *would* have the keys. He said, "*I have the keys.*" Whether or not this new heaven already exists and is waiting for us at death or whether it is some monumental event of the future is immaterial to me. The New Testament claims it is the place where believers will spend eternity.

Satan has been defeated. That is Revelation's promise and our daily strength in a world gone utterly crazy. Jesus has won, and his grace endures forever. As John ends Revelation, so I end:

> *He who testifies these things says, "Yes, I come quickly." Amen! Yes, come, Lord Jesus. The grace of the Lord Jesus Christ be with all the saints. Amen.*
>
> —Rev. 22:20–21

---◆---

LEADERSHIP
(AND EVEN MORE)

Yahweh's word came to me, saying, "Son of man, prophesy against the shepherds of Israel. Prophesy, and tell them, even the shepherds, 'The Lord Yahweh says: "Woe to the shepherds of Israel who feed themselves! Shouldn't the shepherds feed the sheep? You eat the fat. You clothe yourself with the wool. You kill the fatlings, but you don't feed the sheep. You haven't strengthened the diseased. You haven't healed that which was sick. You haven't bound up that which was broken. You haven't brought back that which was driven away. You haven't sought that which was lost, but you have ruled over them with force and with rigor. They were scattered, because there was no shepherd. They became food to all the animals of the field, and were scattered. My sheep wandered through all the mountains, and on every high hill. Yes, my sheep were scattered on all the surface of the earth. There was no one who searched or sought."

"'Therefore, you shepherds, hear Yahweh's word: "As I live," says the Lord Yahweh, "surely because my sheep became a prey, and my sheep became food to all the animals of the field, because there was no shepherd, and my shepherds didn't search for my sheep, but the shepherds fed themselves, and didn't feed my sheep." Therefore, you shepherds, hear Yahweh's word: The Lord Yahweh says: "Behold, I am against

the shepherds. I will require my sheep at their hand, and cause them to cease from feeding the sheep. The shepherds won't feed themselves any more. I will deliver my sheep from their mouth, that they may not be food for them."

"'For the Lord Yahweh says: "Behold, I myself, even I, will search for my sheep, and will seek them out. As a shepherd seeks out his flock in the day that he is among his sheep that are scattered abroad, so I will seek out my sheep. I will deliver them out of all places where they have been scattered in the cloudy and dark day. I will bring them out from the peoples, and gather them from the countries, and will bring them into their own land. I will feed them on the mountains of Israel, by the watercourses, and in all the inhabited places of the country. I will feed them with good pasture; and their fold will be on the mountains of the height of Israel. There they will lie down in a good fold. They will feed on fat pasture on the mountains of Israel. I myself will be the shepherd of my sheep, and I will cause them to lie down," says the Lord Yahweh. "I will seek that which was lost, and will bring back that which was driven away, and will bind up that which was broken, and will strengthen that which was sick; but I will destroy the fat and the strong. I will feed them in justice."'

"As for you, O my flock, the Lord Yahweh says: 'Behold, I judge between sheep and sheep, the rams and the male goats. Does it seem a small thing to you to have fed on the good pasture, but you must tread down with your feet the residue of your pasture? And to have drunk of the clear waters, but must you foul the residue with your feet? As for my sheep, they eat that which you have trodden with your feet, and they drink that which you have fouled with your feet.'

"Therefore the Lord Yahweh says to them: 'Behold, I, even I, will judge between the fat sheep and the lean sheep. Because you thrust with side and with shoulder, and push *all the diseased with your horns, until you have scattered them abroad; therefore I will save my flock, and they will no more be a prey. I will judge between sheep and sheep. I will set up one shepherd over them, and he will feed them, even my servant David. He will feed them, and he will be their shepherd. I, Yahweh, will be their God, and my servant David prince among them. I, Yahweh, have spoken it.*

"I will make with them a covenant of peace, and will cause evil animals to cease out of the land. They will dwell securely in the wilderness, and sleep in the woods. I will make them and the places around my hill a blessing. I will cause the shower to come down in its season. There will be showers of blessing. The tree of the field will yield its fruit, and the earth will yield its increase, and they will be secure in their land. Then they will know that I am Yahweh, when I have broken the bars of their yoke, and have delivered them out of the hand of those who made slaves of them. They will no more be a prey to the nations, neither will the animals of the earth devour them; but they will dwell securely, and no one will make them afraid. I will raise up to them a plantation for renown, and they will no more be consumed with famine in the land, and not bear the shame of the nations any more. They will know that I, Yahweh, their God am with them, and that they, the house of Israel, are my people, says the Lord Yahweh. You my sheep, the sheep of my pasture, are men, and I am your God,' says the Lord Yahweh."

—Ezek. 34:1–31

My daily reading of the Holy Bible is a steady journey through the books, beginning in the Old Testament. I must confess that Jeremiah and Ezekiel are more like endurance races. The repetitive prophesies for Israel to repent from following other gods and return to the one true God is, well, repetitive. Maybe there is a lesson in that sentence. How many times do we have to be told something before we listen? Imagine my surprise when I was reading Ezekiel 34 and God told me to write this chapter.

God's word to me from Ezekiel 34 is *leadership*. He put in my mind three areas of leadership: the church, business and government, and home. I want to apply this chapter to each of those areas. Chapter 34 begins as an admonition to the shepherds of Israel (the priests). Ezekiel accuses them of feeding themselves with the fat and clothing themselves with the wool, all without real care for the flock. He tells them they have not provided for the sick or sought the lost and that they have ruled with cruelty and force. As a result, the flock has been scattered and become food for the beasts of the field. Ezekiel then tells them that God will hold them accountable for their lack of "shepherding."

God appointed members of the tribe of Levi to serve as the priests of the people. Because they were to serve others, they didn't have responsibilities as farmers and ranchers. They had to live off the offerings brought to the tabernacle. In much the same way, ministers today generally don't have duties beyond the ministry. In Ezekiel's day, the priests turned from their teaching and service, yet they were still living off the provisions of the people. In other words, they were feeding themselves first. They did not heal the sick, bind up the wounded, or seek the lost. They allowed the people (sheep) to lead themselves right into the worship of false gods.

Let's bring this to today, starting with the ministers and teachers in the church. Over the last 40 years, we have lost our anchor—the Word. Many church leaders have taken soft stances on tough issues to avoid alienating and therefore losing members. They have allowed society to lead them right into the worship of false gods. Is it the role of the ministers and teachers to share the Word, not soften it to avoid hurting anyone? In my Sunday school class in a previous community, we used to joke about "just leaving that verse out" when it was tough or hit too close to home. Some verses of the Holy Bible are just tough. For example, Jesus says, *"Ask, and it will be given you"* (Matt. 7:7). What does it mean, then, when you feel your prayers aren't answered? We too often find excuses like these for those situations: "Well, God always answers, but sometimes he says no," or "That was just for the disciples; it doesn't apply to us." But could it be that we are not in God's will when we pray? Ministers and teachers (shepherds) are required to hold the sheep accountable so they will not scatter. Our church shepherds must get the sheep back into the Word because the sheep need to know it and understand the intricacies of God's power and plan.

It's very easy to compare the shepherds in Ezekiel to our leaders today, specifically in government and business, but also to anyone who sets policy for those under their authority. Clearly, in most every instance, the professional politicians of today are eating the "*fat*," clothing themselves in the "*wool*," and "*slaughtering the fatlings*," yet they have not "*strengthened the diseased*." We see the same neglect in corporations, unions, and colleges and universities where we find scandals, bribery, corruption, excessive compensation, golden parachutes, and good-ol'-boy networks. Getting to the top is one thing; staying there is quite another. What are leaders willing to do to stay in power? When they confront a hard decision, can they put aside what is best for them personally and instead look out for the best interest of the organization or people below them? Often the action that will lead to short-term gain (quarterly bonus or favor to a loyal subject, for example) is not in the best long-term interest. Leaders must remember that their organization is bigger than they are. They must have compassion and true empathy for their employees and customers and at the same time provide clear, consistent, and positive direction.

Finally, what about shepherding in the home? Today's families are too often scattered, and we all know multiple reasons why—divorce, death, drugs, prison, and careers are a few examples. Some family shepherds have sheep they did not plan for and may not even want. Some family shepherds are ill-prepared financially, mentally, or physically. The breakdown of the family unit and the worship of other gods are the largest contributors to our state of things today. True and caring shepherding in the home is often nonexistent.

God, through Ezekiel, chastised the shepherds (leaders). "*My sheep became a prey*" refers to the lost souls who have not found Christ or have wandered away from the church without being noticed. *"I am against the shepherds. I will require my sheep at their hand, and cause them to cease from feeding the sheep. The shepherds won't feed themselves any more"* (Ezek. 34:10). These are strong words of caution to our leaders in churches, organizations, businesses, corporations, schools, universities, and families. Leaders who feed themselves first without regard to their congregation, organization, or family will be put out of a leadership role.

> *Then whoever hears the sound of the trumpet, and doesn't heed the warning, if the sword comes, and takes him away, his blood will be on his own head. . . . But if the watchman sees the sword come, and doesn't blow the trumpet, and the people aren't warned, and the sword comes, and takes any person from among them; he is taken away in his iniquity, but his blood I will require at the watchman's hand.*
>
> —Ezek. 33:4, 6

Leaders are responsible for what happens to their people. Period.

But God has a plan. In Ezekiel 34:11, God disclosed that he will take over as shepherd and do all the tasks the earthly shepherds have not done. He will rescue his sheep, feed them with good pasture, find and bring back the lost, bind up the injured, and strengthen the weak.

Here's my challenge for today's church leaders. Rescue those who have wandered away, feed the hungry (physically, but more specifically spiritually), serve those with truth who have been wounded within the church, and give hope to those who have yet to find peace in Jesus.

Here's my challenge for today's government and business leaders. Stop working to preserve your own power. Work for those under you, lift up the least in your organization, and provide real vision and direction with goals to strengthen not only your organization but those your organization serves.

Here's my challenge for today's leaders in the home. Take family seriously, and don't just play at it. Put aside differences, and hold the family together. Teach your family strong values and faith in Christ, and help them understand God's Word. Provide emotional, physical, and financial support for your family. Don't assume they are better off without you. As a good shepherd does not leave the gate unattended for wolves and thieves to come in, so good family shepherds will not leave the gates of the minds of their children open to be filled by the world.

God will judge between good shepherds and bad shepherds. (Many who call themselves modern-day prophets describe the current events of the world as a contemporary call from God to his people to return to him. They say, and rightly so, that we have turned our faces to other gods—money and other wealth, entertainment, and false or even no teaching. In their proclamation, God is begging and pleading for us to realize that without him as our Lord, we have no peace or comfort. But God promises one good shepherd, Jesus Christ. With Jesus as the shepherd, God will make a covenant of peace (peace in this case is contentment in our situation resulting from our relationship with Jesus). Jesus will send showers of blessing, fruit and increase, security, freedom, and safety. Significantly in today's climate, he will take away fear *if* we look to him.

Thank you, Jesus, for being the perfect Shepherd!

---·❖·---

WHAT DO
OTHERS SEE?

It pleased Darius to set over the kingdom one hundred twenty local governors, who should be throughout the whole kingdom; and over them three presidents, of whom Daniel was one; that these local governors might give account to them, and that the king should suffer no loss. Then this Daniel was distinguished above the presidents and the local governors, because an excellent spirit was in him; and the king thought to set him over the whole realm.

Then the presidents and the local governors sought to find occasion against Daniel as touching the kingdom; but they could find no occasion or fault, because he was faithful. There wasn't any error or fault found in him. Then these men said, "We won't find any occasion against this Daniel, unless we find it against him concerning the law of his God."

Then these presidents and local governors assembled together to the king, and said this to him, "King Darius, live forever! All the presidents of the kingdom, the deputies and the local governors, the counselors and the governors, have consulted together to establish a royal statute, and to make a strong decree, that whoever asks a petition of any god or man for thirty days, except of you, O king, he shall be cast into the den of lions. Now, O king, establish the decree, and sign the writing, that it not be changed, according to the law of the Medes and Persians, which doesn't alter." Therefore king Darius signed the writing and the decree.

When Daniel knew that the writing was signed, he went into his house (now his windows were open in his room toward Jerusalem) and he kneeled on his knees three times a day, and prayed, and gave thanks before his God, as he did before. Then these men assembled together, and found Daniel making petition and supplication before his God. Then they came near, and spoke before the king concerning the king's decree: "Haven't you signed a decree that every man who makes a petition to any god or man within thirty days, except to you, O king, shall be cast into the den of lions?"

The king answered, "This thing is true, according to the law of the Medes and Persians, which doesn't alter."

Then they answered and said before the king, "That Daniel, who is of the children of the captivity of Judah, doesn't respect you, O king, nor the decree that you have signed, but makes his petition three times a day." Then the king, when he heard these words, was very displeased, and set his heart on Daniel to deliver him; and he labored until the going down of the sun to rescue him.

Then these men assembled together to the king, and said to the king, "Know, O king, that it is a law of the Medes and Persians, that no decree nor statute which the king establishes may be changed."

Then the king commanded, and they brought Daniel, and cast him into the den of lions. The king spoke and said to Daniel, "Your God whom you serve continually, he will deliver you."

A stone was brought, and laid on the mouth of the den; and the king sealed it with his own signet, and with the signet of his lords; that nothing might be changed concerning Daniel.

Then the king went to his palace, and passed the night fasting. No musical instruments were brought before him; and his sleep fled from him.

Then the king arose very early in the morning, and went in haste to the den of lions. When he came near to the den to Daniel, he cried with a troubled voice. The king spoke and said to Daniel, "Daniel, servant of the living God, is your God, whom you serve continually, able to deliver you from the lions?"

Then Daniel said to the king, "O king, live forever! My God has sent his angel, and has shut the lions' mouths, and they have not hurt me; because as before him innocence was found in me; and also before you, O king, I have done no harm."

Then the king was exceedingly glad, and commanded that they should take Daniel up out of the den. So Daniel was taken up out of the den, and no kind of harm was found on him, because he had trusted in his God.

The king commanded, and they brought those men who had accused Daniel, and they cast them into the den of lions, them, their children, and their wives; and the lions mauled them, and broke all their bones in pieces, before they came to the bottom of the den.

Then king Darius wrote to all the peoples, nations, and languages, who dwell in all the earth:

"Peace be multiplied to you.

"I make a decree that in all the dominion of my kingdom men tremble and fear before the God of Daniel;

"for he is the living God,
and steadfast forever.
His kingdom is that which will not be destroyed.
His dominion will be even to the end.
He delivers and rescues.

He works signs and wonders in heaven and in earth,
who has delivered Daniel from the power of the lions."
So this Daniel prospered in the reign of Darius, and in the
reign of Cyrus the Persian.

—Dan. 6:1–28

I was fortunate to have grown up in church. Before I learned how to read or solve math problems, I learned the great stories of the Old Testament. Daniel 6 is one of those stories. But now, reading it with more experience, depth, and knowledge some 50 years later, I see more to the story than the simple Daniel in the lion's den story. In fact, I see at least three stories running through the chapter.

The first and most obvious story sets the stage for the other two. Daniel was and had been an incredible servant of God his entire life. Based on historical records of the reigns of the various kings to whom Daniel provided counsel, Daniel was approximately 80 years old when the events in this chapter took place. Many might say that Daniel had a good long life and had nothing to lose. I say that Daniel had a good long life, and he *knew* he had nothing to lose.

Of course, as revealed in the scripture above, Daniel defied the king's rule to cease worship of anything or any god except the king for a 30-day period. Knowing that the king had signed the decree and that the penalty for defying that decree was a visit to the lions' den, Daniel continued his daily tradition of praying to God three times—doing so deliberately in public where his act of honor, respect, thanksgiving, and love for God were a testimony to those around him. Daniel knew he had nothing to lose and everything to gain because he had experienced it multiple times during his life. Daniel had interpreted (and even recalled) the king's dreams when no one else could. He had seen his three close friends (Shadrach, Meshach, and Abednego) thrown into a seven-times heated furnace and not only come out of the furnace, but also come out of the furnace without even the smell of smoke. Daniel had read the handwriting on the wall. For Daniel to consider neither his own life nor the consequences of his action was a habit. In fact, his habit is what got him into this position in the first place.

And that leads to story number two.

Daniel, the captive, had been set above almost all other rulers in Babylon. He was one of three presidents set over the satraps (a provincial or local ruler). But Daniel stood above the other two presidents and all the satraps because *"an excellent spirit was in him,"* and the king appointed him over the whole kingdom. This promotion brought the others to jealousy, and they sought *"occasion"* against Daniel. Try as they might, they could not find a fault, error, or mistake in Daniel's handling of the king's affairs. But—and this goes directly to the title and ultimate point of this writing—they knew Daniel would worship God without exception. They saw Daniel's commitment to God, and they bet on it. The decree of the king to worship no one else but him was a trap, and they had 100 percent confidence that Daniel would walk right into it. They followed Daniel's routine and caught him worshiping and praising God, just as they knew he would.

The third story is of King Darius who respected and trusted Daniel. He had full confidence in Daniel because he had seen Daniel's actions. He placed Daniel over the whole kingdom. But like so many of us, Darius allowed other presidents and satraps to play on his pride and lead him into a bad decision that defied his better judgment. They reminded Darius that he was in charge and should be honored—solely. Darius lost his logic, put himself first, and made a worthless decision. When the presidents and satraps caught Daniel and brought it to Darius's attention, he was trapped. Darius knew he had made a serious mistake, and he regretted his decree, but he was bound by his own words.

Interestingly, when Darius ordered Daniel into the lion's den, he did so with these words: *"Your God whom you serve continually, he will deliver you."* Darius had seen Daniel's actions and God's faithfulness to Daniel. Darius didn't sleep all night. He fasted and returned to the lion's den early in the morning, perhaps expecting or at least hoping to find Daniel unharmed. He called out, *"Daniel, servant of the living God, is your*

God, whom you serve continually, able to deliver you from the lions?" I think he was expecting to hear Daniel's voice, although not necessarily the response he heard: "O king, live forever! My God has sent his angel, and has shut the lions' mouths, and they have not hurt me; because as before him innocence was found in me; and also before you, O king, I have done no harm."

With exceeding joy, Darius made a new decree. Everyone in the kingdom must tremble before the God of Daniel, the one true God, "for he is the living God, and steadfast forever. His kingdom is that which will not be destroyed. His dominion will be even to the end." Darius's pride was gone, inspired by the faith and follow-through of Daniel.

We can ask these questions: What do others see when they see us? Do our actions consistently prove our love for God? Do others know we love God? If the government ordered us to cease worshiping God, would we do it? Knowing the punishment would be a den of lions, could we open our windows and show the world our devotion to the one true God? Our actions tell others who we are. Daniel was a man of honor and integrity, through and through.

I fear that Daniel 5:27 sometimes describes me: "You are weighed in the balances, and are found wanting." I know no person who can balance their own scale, but I do know someone who can balance the scale for us—Jesus. He knew that following God's will would lead to his death, but he obeyed and balanced our scales. With Jesus, we will never be found wanting. Alleluia!

---❖---

JUST
BELIEVE

But as many as received him, to them he gave the right to become God's children, to those who believe in his name: who were born not of blood, nor of the will of the flesh, nor of the will of man, but of God.

—John 1:12–13

For God so loved the world, that he gave his one and only Son, that whoever believes in him should not perish, but have eternal life.

—John 3:16

Jesus answered them, "This is the work of God, that you believe in him whom he has sent."

—John 6:29

Jesus said to them, "I am the bread of life. Whoever comes to me will not be hungry, and whoever believes in me will never be thirsty."

—John 6:35

Jesus said to her, "I am the resurrection and the life. He who believes in me will still live, even if he dies. Whoever lives and believes in me will never die. Do you believe this?"

She said to him, "Yes, Lord. I have come to believe that you are the Christ, God's Son, he who comes into the world."

—John 11:25–27

Jesus said to her, "Didn't I tell you that if you believed, you would see God's glory?"

—John 11:40

But these are written, that you may believe that Jesus is the Christ, the Son of God, and that believing you may have life in his name.

—John 20:31

Whom, not having known, you love. In him, though now you don't see him, yet believing, you rejoice greatly with joy that is unspeakable and full of glory, receiving the result of your faith, the salvation of your souls.

—1 Pet. 1:8–9

Coming into his own country, he taught them in their synagogue, so that they were astonished and said, "Where did this man get this wisdom and these mighty works? Isn't this the carpenter's son? Isn't his mother called Mary, and his brothers James, Joses, Simon, and Judas? Aren't all of his sisters with us? Where then did this man get all of these things?" They were offended by him.

But Jesus said to them, "A prophet is not without honor, except in his own country and in his own house." He didn't do many mighty works there because of their unbelief.

—Matt. 13:54–58

When they came to the multitude, a man came to him, kneeling down to him and saying, "Lord, have mercy on my son, for he is epileptic and suffers grievously; for he often falls into the fire, and often into the water. So I brought him to your disciples, and they could not cure him."

Jesus answered, "Faithless and perverse generation! How long will I be with you? How long will I bear with you? Bring him here to me." Jesus rebuked the demon, and it went out of him, and the boy was cured from that hour.

Then the disciples came to Jesus privately, and said, "Why weren't we able to cast it out?"

He said to them, "Because of your unbelief. For most certainly I tell you, if you have faith as a grain of mustard seed, you will tell this mountain, 'Move from here to there,' and it will move; and nothing will be impossible for you. But this kind doesn't go out except by prayer and fasting."

—Matt. 17:14–21

Jesus answered them, "Most certainly I tell you, if you have faith and don't doubt, you will not only do what was done to the fig tree, but even if you told this mountain, 'Be taken up and cast into the sea,' it would be done. All things, whatever you ask in prayer, believing, you will receive."

—Matt. 21:21–22

But Jesus hearing it, answered him, "Don't be afraid. Only believe, and she will be healed."

—Luke 8:50

But let him ask in faith, without any doubting, for he who doubts is like a wave of the sea, driven by the wind and tossed.

—James 1:6

While we don't look at the things which are seen, but at the things which are not seen. For the things which are seen are temporal, but the things which are not seen are eternal.

—2 Cor. 4:18

You believe that God is one. You do well. The demons also believe, and shudder.

—James 2:19

So faith comes by hearing, and hearing by the word of God.
—Rom. 10:17

For with the heart, one believes resulting in righteousness; and with the mouth confession is made resulting in salvation. For the Scripture says, "Whoever believes in him will not be disappointed."
—Rom. 10:10–11

But having the same spirit of faith, according to that which is written, "I believed, and therefore I spoke." We also believe, and therefore we also speak.
—2 Cor. 4:13

According to the *Merriam-Webster* online dictionary, the word *believe* means "to consider to be true or honest; to accept the word or evidence of; to hold as an opinion, to accept something as true, genuine, or real; to have a firm or wholehearted religious conviction or persuasion; to have a firm conviction as to the goodness, efficacy, or ability of something."

Christians easily grasp belief and completely miss it at the same time. Let me try to explain by dividing the scriptures into three topical sections. The definition of *believe* ranges from holding an opinion to having firm conviction to having wholehearted religious conviction. Arguably, we have degrees of belief. In other words, there are some things we believe with more commitment than others.

The scriptures in the first group explain believing in Jesus for our salvation. This belief is a basic tenet of Christianity. In making our confession, we affirm our belief that Jesus is the Son of God who came to earth in human form to live among us, to suffer as one of us, to take on all our sins, to die for us, and ultimately to be raised from the grave and live forever—a precious and miraculous story verifying that Jesus is absolutely unique. There are no other examples in history or any other religion of a man who claimed to be the Son of God, performed miracles, sacrificed his own life to save the world, and rose from the dead. Though the unbelieving may call Jesus's story preposterous, Christians solidly believe it.

The scriptures in the second group of verses explain unbelief. In Matthew 13, Jesus was in his hometown, talking to people who had known him his entire life. They knew his family, his childhood, and his carpentry. They didn't believe him because he had grown up among them, and they believed he was as commonplace as the rest of them. They were thinking of him only from a natural perspective.

In Matthew 17, the disciples couldn't heal a man with seizures. When Jesus arrived, he immediately rebuked the demon, leaving the young man healed of his seizures. When the disciples asked why they had not been able to cast out the demon, Jesus replied, *"Because of your unbelief."* In verse 21, Jesus says, *"But this kind doesn't go out except by prayer and fasting."* This kind of what? This kind of unbelief. In Mark, a similar passage, the father of the young man cried out, *"Help my unbelief!"* (Mark 9:24). In two related passages from Matthew and Mark 11, Jesus says that with faith, you can throw a mountain into the sea, if only you have no doubt. Finally, in a passage from Luke, Jesus states, *"Don't be afraid. Only believe"* (Luke 8:50).

Are we not similar to the disciples? While we wholeheartedly accept Christ's salvation, we dismiss his healing, resurrecting, protecting power in our lives. You may say, "Yes, there are many great stories about what Jesus did in the past, but what about now? Do miracles happen today? What role do we play in those miracles?"

The third group of scriptures adds some context. It begins with a passage from James, who described a doubtful person as one being tossed by the wind. In 2 Corinthians, Paul suggests that our faith is based not on what we can see but on what we can't see. We accept Christ as our Savior, but we struggle with faith in practice. We let what we see in the natural world around us have greater influence on our beliefs, allowing doubt to creep into our minds. A little doubt is a mighty force.

We are conditioned by our history, just as the citizens from Jesus's hometown were. We have not seen a fig tree cursed and withered or a mountain moved at another's command. The evidence around us says that our belief in Jesus's power today is unfounded and even foolish. But it takes more than a belief in the historical acts of Jesus to feel his power today. Even the demons believe (James 2:19).

How do we just believe? Simply put, we need to change the dominant influences in our lives. If our most dominant influence is what we see, we will believe we are bound by nature, and we will doubt. If we believe in the doom-and-gloom news reports that sell advertising for networks, newspapers, and online news outlets, we will not expect the power of Jesus to shine in our lives. But Paul gives us a direction to change your influence. He says, *"So faith comes by hearing, and hearing by the word of God"* (Rom. 10:17).

We have to be in the Word regularly in order to overcome the influences of nature. Our senses are very powerful. In fact, our senses were developed in us by God to keep us alive. Since the fall of Adam and Eve, we have needed our sight to see dangerous situations, our hearing to be aware of our surroundings, our smell and taste to know what is not good for us, and our touch to feel pain. But given no other direction, our senses will make us fearful because that is what they are designed to do. But we are to live in the Spirit. Our spirit is our direct connection to God. Our spirit has to be the dominant part of our being. To make it dominant, we have to feed it with God's Word. As Jesus said, unbelief will go away only through study, prayer, and fasting. We have to focus on God.

The Bible also tells us there is power in what we say. Proverbs 18:21 says, *"Death and life are in the power of the tongue; those who love it will eat its fruit."* The two passages in Romans and 2 Corinthians at the beginning of this chapter explain the power of speaking our faith. Jesus spoke to the fig tree. Jesus said to command the mountain. If we believe in our minds but speak doom and gloom from our mouths, we counteract our thinking. Hearing is a powerful sense. What can you expect of your mind if its dominant influence is your own negative voice in your ear?

"Just believe" is not quite as simple as it sounds. We have to change our dominant influence. If that is God's Word, our spirit within us will take control and open us ever deeper to God's dominant influence. When we are born again, we are given a new, perfect spirit (Gal. 4:6; 1 Cor. 3:16). We have to let that perfect spirit within us dominate our body and soul, our soul being our mind, will, and emotions. We're not made to do this life alone. Allow him in.

> *Behold, I stand at the door and knock. If anyone hears my voice and opens the door, then I will come in to him, and will dine with him, and he with me.*
>
> —Rev. 3:20

---❖---

CONSIDER
YOUR WAYS

Now therefore this is what Yahweh of Armies says: "Consider your ways. You have sown much, and bring in little. You eat, but you don't have enough. You drink, but you aren't filled with drink. You clothe yourselves, but no one is warm, and he who earns wages earns wages to put them into a bag with holes in it."

This is what Yahweh of Armies says: "Consider your ways. Go up to the mountain, bring wood, and build the house. I will take pleasure in it, and I will be glorified," says Yahweh. "You looked for much, and, behold, it came to little; and when you brought it home, I blew it away. Why?" says Yahweh of Armies, "Because of my house that lies waste, while each of you is busy with his own house."

—Hag. 1:5–9

God sent most of the children of Israel into Babylonian captivity, but he kept a remnant behind. Most of the Old Testament prophets are speaking of this event, and the books of Kings and Chronicles cover some of the details. Each said that one day Israel would return and build a house to the Lord. Ezra and Nehemiah wrote about rebuilding the temple and the city walls. Haggai wrote about building the house of God. The people were commanded to rebuild, but they were making excuses. Haggai's charge was to get them on task, or at least let them know they had no excuses.

I see in these verses a more contemporary setting. Our lives are supposed to be intentional and purposeful. To consider your ways is to pick a path with thought and discernment. That path could be the literal path on which you are walking or the figurative influence in your life. Let's focus on the latter and suggest that God is telling us to consider our beliefs and influences. Do we wholeheartedly believe his Word? Do we pick and choose which verses to honor and which to ignore? Do we allow his Word to guide our daily decisions? Are we more influenced by the unsaved world around us? Do we believe only what we can see, hear, smell, taste, and feel? Give careful, deliberate, and discerning consideration to your ways.

> *You have sown much, and bring in little. You eat, but you don't have enough. You drink, but you aren't filled with drink. You clothe yourselves, but no one is warm, and he who earns wages earns wages to put them into a bag with holes in it.*
>
> —Hag. 1:6

God has plans for each of us (Jer. 29:11), but we have to listen to hear them. Are we listening for God's purpose for us, or did we make up our own mind long ago, and, by golly, that's the direction we're headed? When we're out of God's will for our lives, we're wasting our time. One of my favorite sayings is "the harder I work, the behinder I get." This saying applies to our lives outside of God's will. We may be busy, but we aren't fulfilled in the busyness (or business). We don't find satisfaction, energy, or even financial reward. No matter what we do, we feel empty. No matter what we do, we can't seem to get ahead or even caught up. Our days feel pointless. There is a hole. I bet if you look very closely, you will find that hole is just the size of Jesus. Accepting his grace doesn't make us perfect, but it does make us forgiven. Accepting his lordship will take us beyond forgiven, and it will fill that hole. It will give us energy, fulfillment, satisfaction, and purpose. However, accepting his lordship means giving up the most influential person we know—ourselves. To allow him to rule, we have to suppress our own wants and desires. As I said in an earlier chapter, we have to allow our perfect spirit to have the final say. We must consider our ways.

"Go up to the mountain, bring wood, and build the house. I will take pleasure in it, and I will be glorified," says Yahweh.
—Hag. 1:8

We must deliberately invite him in and make a place for him to live inside us. When we live without considering him in all our ways, we tend to view his ways as an invasion of our personal desires. But if we build a home for him in our hearts, his desires become our desires without conflict. This I guarantee: If you honor him by building him a place in your heart, he will take pleasure in it. Consider your ways.

"Why?" says Yahweh of Armies, "Because of my house that lies waste, while each of you is busy with his own house."
—Hag. 1:9

This sentence is the culmination of the passage. Why do we plant but not harvest? Why do we eat and remain hungry? Why do we not feel filled? It's because our influences and priorities are misplaced.

The words *my house* can mean two different things. The first meaning might be God's house—the church. I'm not talking about the building but rather the body of the church. Too many churches forsake the full meaning of God's Word and focus solely on the few verses that encourage salvation. I'm certainly not opposed to salvation, of course—it's good for the soul (ha ha). But salvation, although the most critical and important step in our relationship with God, is not the end. Christians are called to do more than just make converts to Jesus; they are called to make disciples—lifetime learners. The church is called to know his Word, believe his Word, teach his Word, and live his Word. The church is called to challenge each of us to grow in our faith and understanding. An average grade may get us into heaven, but shouldn't we all be striving for an A+? The church in the broad sense has tried to make believing so easy that no one has to change in order to belong. But Jesus calls us to change. He calls us to take up our cross and follow him. Consider the ways of the church.

The second meaning of *my house* is the new temple of God—each individual believer. We can build his house inside us, or we can seek our own desires. Here is another guarantee: If we put ourselves first, building homes that we want, his house inside us will be in ruin, possibly unbuilt. We simply can't divide our loyalties that way. We either build our own house or we build his house. If we build our house, we will run out of time, materials, and energy to build his house. But if we build his house, he will have room for us to move in with him!

This is what Yahweh of Armies says: "Consider your ways."
—Hag. 1:7

WHO
ARE WE?

Then Jesus was led up by the Spirit into the wilderness to be tempted by the devil. When he had fasted forty days and forty nights, he was hungry afterward. The tempter came and said to him, "If you are the Son of God, command that these stones become bread."

But he answered, "It is written, 'Man shall not live by bread alone, but by every word that proceeds out of God's mouth.'"

Then the devil took him into the holy city. He set him on the pinnacle of the temple, and said to him, "If you are the Son of God, throw yourself down, for it is written,

> *'He will command his angels concerning you,' and,*
> *'On their hands they will bear you up,*
> > *so that you don't dash your foot against a stone.'"*

Jesus said to him, "Again, it is written, 'You shall not test the Lord, your God.'"

Again, the devil took him to an exceedingly high mountain, and showed him all the kingdoms of the world and their glory. He said to him, "I will give you all of these things, if you will fall down and worship me."

Then Jesus said to him, "Get behind me, Satan! For it is written, 'You shall worship the Lord your God, and you shall serve him only.'"

Then the devil left him, and behold, angels came and served him.

—Matt. 4:1–11

Jesus was tempted three times by the devil. First John 2:15–16 says. *"Don't love the world or the things that are in the world. If anyone loves the world, the Father's love isn't in him. For all that is in the world, the lust of the flesh, the lust of the eyes, and the pride of life, isn't the Father's, but is the world's."* Jesus was tempted in all three of these areas. But my study suggested a fourth temptation: doubt. You see, two of the three temptations begin, *"If you are the Son of God."* This is a significant temptation and one the devil regularly uses against us.

Jesus was baptized right before this time of temptation, but he had yet to begin his public ministry or perform miracles. If at any point in his life he could have been tempted with doubt, this was certainly a good time for the devil to try. By saying "if you are," Satan was introducing the concept of doubt. He was asking Jesus, "How do you know you are the Son of God? Are you sure?"

Does Satan not come at us with the same temptation? Does he not try to make us doubt who we are in Christ? The devil might say, "How do you know you are a child of God? Can you see, smell, touch, hear, or taste proof? What have you ever done to deserve all this? Do you really think you are worthy of God's attention, care, healing, salvation, and love? What difference does being a Christian really make? Wouldn't it be easier just to be and think like everyone else?"

Jesus knew he was God's Son and responded to the tempter each time by confidently quoting scripture. We, too, should have that same knowledge and confidence—two things that will empower us to fend off the devil. But how do we know?

Behold, I give you authority to tread on serpents and scorpions, and over all the power of the enemy. Nothing will in any way hurt you.

—Luke 10:19

Therefore if anyone is in Christ, he is a new creation. The old things have passed away. Behold, all things have become new.

—2 Cor. 5:17

My God will supply every need of yours according to his riches in glory in Christ Jesus.

—Phil. 4:19

And if children, then heirs: heirs of God and joint heirs with Christ, if indeed we suffer with him, that we may also be glorified with him.

—Rom. 8:17

For him who knew no sin he made to be sin on our behalf; so that in him we might become the righteousness of God.

—2 Cor. 5:21

Some of you were such, but you were washed. But you were sanctified. But you were justified in the name of the Lord Jesus, and in the Spirit of our God.

—1 Cor. 6:11

We were buried therefore with him through baptism into death, that just as Christ was raised from the dead through the glory of the Father, so we also might walk in newness of life.

—Rom. 6:4

For the wages of sin is death, but the free gift of God is eternal life in Christ Jesus our Lord.

—Rom. 6:23

Being confident of this very thing, that he who began a good work in you will complete it until the day of Jesus Christ.

—Phil. 1:6

He who has the Son has the life. He who doesn't have God's Son doesn't have the life.

—1 John 5:12

For by grace you have been saved through faith, and that not of yourselves; it is the gift of God, not of works, that no one would boast.

—Eph. 2:8–9

Humble yourselves therefore under the mighty hand of God, that he may exalt you in due time, casting all your worries on him, because he cares for you.

 Be sober and self-controlled. Be watchful. Your adversary, the devil, walks around like a roaring lion, seeking whom he may devour. Withstand him steadfast in your faith, knowing that your brothers who are in the world are undergoing the same sufferings. But may the God of all grace, who called you to his eternal glory by Christ Jesus, after you have suffered a little while, perfect, establish, strengthen, and settle you. To him be the glory and the power forever and ever. Amen.

—1 Pet. 5:6–11

But be doers of the word, and not only hearers, deluding your own selves. For if anyone is a hearer of the word and not a doer, he is like a man looking at his natural face in a mirror; for he sees himself, and goes away, and immediately forgets what kind of man he was. But he who looks into the perfect law of freedom and continues, not being a hearer who forgets, but a doer of the work, this man will be blessed in what he does.

—James 1:22–25

Put on therefore, as God's chosen ones, holy and beloved, a heart of compassion, kindness, lowliness, humility, and perseverance; bearing with one another, and forgiving each other, if any man has a complaint against any; even as Christ forgave you, so you also do.

Above all these things, walk in love, which is the bond of perfection. And let the peace of God rule in your hearts, to which also you were called in one body, and be thankful. Let the word of Christ dwell in you richly; in all wisdom teaching and admonishing one another with psalms, hymns, and spiritual songs, singing with grace in your heart to the Lord.

Whatever you do, in word or in deed, do all in the name of the Lord Jesus, giving thanks to God the Father, through him.

—Col. 3:12–17

Most certainly I tell you, he who believes in me, the works that I do, he will do also; and he will do greater works than these, because I am going to my Father.

—John 14:12

Who are we? We are the children of God! And we can confidently claim the righteousness of Jesus by grace, through faith, as joint heirs of the Father.

---❖---

LET YOUR
WILL BE DONE

Let your Kingdom come.
    Let your will be done on earth as it is in heaven.
                                 —Matt. 6:10

In the Sermon on the Mount, Jesus teaches a range of topics. One of the more important lessons is how to pray. The Lord's Prayer, as we know it, was not a symbolic prayer to repeat without thought but rather a model prayer that showed us these elements to include in a prayer:

1. God should be honored above all.
2. God's will shall be done on earth and in heaven.
3. God supplies our daily needs.
4. We request forgiveness of our sins.
5. God can deliver us.

The focus of this chapter is on point two: God's will and his kingdom here and now. As we pray for God's kingdom to come, what are we asking for? Luke 17:20–21 says, *"Being asked by the Pharisees when God's Kingdom would come, he answered them, 'God's Kingdom doesn't come with observation; neither will they say, "Look, here!" or, "Look, there!" for behold, God's Kingdom is within you.'"* While the Jews were awaiting a political kingdom on earth, Jesus told them that the kingdom of God dwells among us in our hearts. We will not find comfort, peace, or sustenance in people or people's organizations or programs, but only through God's guidance in our individual lives. By praying for God's kingdom to come, we are asking God to live within us, to be our Lord and Master, to be the dominate influence in our lives. And by extension, we must pray that God's kingdom expands through the salvation of all people. What greater petition could we make than asking his voice to be the dominant influence in all hearts?

In the same manner, we must ask that his will be done in our individual lives. But what is God's will? Scripture gives us a clear picture of what God intends for each of us. He gave us authority and dominion over the earth.

> God said, "Let's make man in our image, after our likeness. Let them have dominion over the fish of the sea, and over the birds of the sky, and over the livestock, and over all the earth, and over every creeping thing that creeps on the earth." God created man in his own image. In God's image he created him; male and female he created them. God blessed them. God said to them, "Be fruitful, multiply, fill the earth, and subdue it. Have dominion over the fish of the sea, over the birds of the sky, and over every living thing that moves on the earth." God said, "Behold, I have given you every herb yielding seed, which is on the surface of all the earth, and every tree, which bears fruit yielding seed. It will be your food. To every animal of the earth, and to every bird of the sky, and to everything that creeps on the earth, in which there is life, I have given every green herb for food;" and it was so.
>
> —Gen. 1:26–30

Similarly, after the flood, Genesis records mankind's authority.

> God blessed Noah and his sons, and said to them, "Be fruitful, multiply, and replenish the earth. The fear of you and the dread of you will be on every animal of the earth, and on every

bird of the sky. Everything that moves along the ground, and
all the fish of the sea, are delivered into your hand."

—Gen. 9:1–2

A psalm expands on this even further.

When I consider your heavens, the work of your fingers,
  the moon and the stars, which you have ordained;
what is man, that you think of him?
  What is the son of man, that you care for him?
For you have made him a little lower than the angels,
  and crowned him with glory and honor.
You make him ruler over the works of your hands.
  You have put all things under his feet:
All sheep and cattle,
  yes, and the animals of the field,
  the birds of the sky, the fish of the sea,
  and whatever passes through the paths of the seas.

—Ps. 8:3–8

Of course, mankind sinned and gave rule of the world to Satan. But
our all-knowing and all-loving God had a plan.

For he didn't subject the world to come, of which we speak, to
angels. But one has somewhere testified, saying,

  "What is man, that you think of him?
    Or the son of man, that you care for him?
  You made him a little lower than the angels.
    You crowned him with glory and honor.
    You have put all things in subjection under his feet."

For in that he subjected all things to him, he left nothing
that is not subject to him. But now we don't see all things
subjected to him, yet. But we see him who has been made a

little lower than the angels, Jesus, because of the suffering of death crowned with glory and honor, that by the grace of God he should taste of death for everyone. For it became him, for whom are all things, and through whom are all things, in bringing many children to glory, to make the author of their salvation perfect through sufferings. For both he who sanctifies and those who are sanctified are all from one, for which cause he is not ashamed to call them brothers, saying,

> *"I will declare your name to my brothers.*
> *Among the congregation I will sing your praise."*

Again, "I will put my trust in him." Again, "Behold, here I am with the children whom God has given me." Since then the children have shared in flesh and blood, he also himself in the same way partook of the same, that through death he might bring to nothing him who had the power of death, that is, the devil, and might deliver all of them who through fear of death were all their lifetime subject to bondage. For most certainly, he doesn't give help to angels, but he gives help to the offspring of Abraham. Therefore he was obligated in all things to be made like his brothers, that he might become a merciful and faithful high priest in things pertaining to God, to make atonement for the sins of the people.

—Heb. 2:5–17

We begin to get a picture of God's will in the Old Testament.

"For I know the thoughts that I think toward you," says Yahweh, "thoughts of peace, and not of evil, to give you hope and a future. You shall call on me, and you shall go and pray to me, and I will listen to you. You shall seek me, and find me, when you search for me with all your heart."

—Jer. 29:11–13

Trust in Yahweh, and do good.
Dwell in the land, and enjoy safe pasture.
Also delight yourself in Yahweh,
and he will give you the desires of your heart.
Commit your way to Yahweh.
Trust also in him, and he will do this:
he will make your righteousness shine out like light,
and your justice as the noon day sun.

—Ps. 37:3–6

Yahweh is my shepherd:
I shall lack nothing.
He makes me lie down in green pastures.
He leads me beside still waters.
He restores my soul.
He guides me in the paths of righteousness for his name's sake.
Even though I walk through the valley of the shadow of death,
I will fear no evil, for you are with me.
Your rod and your staff, they comfort me.
You prepare a table before me in the presence of my enemies.
You anoint my head with oil.
My cup runs over.
Surely goodness and loving kindness shall follow me all the
days of my life,
and I will dwell in Yahweh's house forever.

—Ps. 23:1–6

It is through our Savior that we find God's true will for each person on earth.

For God so loved the world, that he gave his one and only
Son, that whoever believes in him should not perish, but have
eternal life. For God didn't send his Son into the world to judge
the world, but that the world should be saved through him.

—John 3:16–17

For I have come down from heaven, not to do my own will, but the will of him who sent me. This is the will of my Father who sent me, that of all he has given to me I should lose nothing, but should raise him up at the last day. This is the will of the one who sent me, that everyone who sees the Son, and believes in him, should have eternal life; and I will raise him up at the last day.

—John 6:38–40

I exhort therefore, first of all, that petitions, prayers, intercessions, and givings of thanks be made for all men: for kings and all who are in high places, that we may lead a tranquil and quiet life in all godliness and reverence. For this is good and acceptable in the sight of God our Savior, who desires all people to be saved and come to full knowledge of the truth. For there is one God, and one mediator between God and men, the man Christ Jesus.

—1 Tim. 2:1–5

Always rejoice. Pray without ceasing. In everything give thanks, for this is the will of God in Christ Jesus toward you.

—1 Thess. 5:16–18

I can do all things through Christ, who strengthens me.

—Phil. 4:13

And this is expanded through the Holy Spirit.

In the same way, the Spirit also helps our weaknesses, for we don't know how to pray as we ought. But the Spirit himself makes intercession for us with groanings which can't be uttered. He who searches the hearts knows what is on the Spirit's mind, because he makes intercession for the saints according to God.

We know that all things work together for good for those who love God, for those who are called according to his purpose. For whom he foreknew, he also predestined to be conformed to the image of his Son, that he might be the firstborn among many brothers. Whom he predestined, those he also called. Whom he called, those he also justified. Whom he justified, those he also glorified.

—Rom. 8:26–30

And we solidify our knowledge of God's will through more scripture.

Therefore I urge you, brothers, by the mercies of God, to present your bodies a living sacrifice, holy, acceptable to God, which is your spiritual service. Don't be conformed to this world, but be transformed by the renewing of your mind, so that you may prove what is the good, well-pleasing, and perfect will of God.

—Rom. 12:1–2

He has shown you, O man, what is good.
   What does Yahweh require of you, but to act justly,
   to love mercy, and to walk humbly with your God?

—Mic. 6:8

But if any of you lacks wisdom, let him ask of God, who gives to all liberally and without reproach, and it will be given to him.

—James 1:5

We must pray to have God's kingdom and his will here on earth *"as it is in heaven."* This clause begs the question, "How is it in heaven?" Scripture also provides us a great idea of what heaven is like and what God wants for us each day.

In my Father's house are many homes. If it weren't so, I would have told you. I am going to prepare a place for you. If I go and prepare a place for you, I will come again, and will receive you to myself; that where I am, you may be there also. You know where I go, and you know the way.

—John 14:2–4

Don't lay up treasures for yourselves on the earth, where moth and rust consume, and where thieves break through and steal; but lay up for yourselves treasures in heaven, where neither moth nor rust consume, and where thieves don't break through and steal.

—Matt. 6:19–20

They will come from the east, west, north, and south, and will sit down in God's Kingdom. Behold, there are some who are last who will be first, and there are some who are first who will be last.

—Luke 13:29–30

But as it is written,
> *"Things which an eye didn't see, and an ear didn't hear,*
> *which didn't enter into the heart of man,*
> *these God has prepared for those who love him."*

—1 Cor. 2:9

But, according to his promise, we look for new heavens and a new earth, in which righteousness dwells.

—2 Pet. 3:13

But perhaps the most vivid descriptions of heaven come from the revelation to John.

After these things I looked, and behold, a great multitude, which no man could count, out of every nation and of all tribes, peoples, and languages, standing before the throne and before the Lamb, dressed in white robes, with palm branches in their hands. They cried with a loud voice, saying, "Salvation be to our God, who sits on the throne, and to the Lamb!"

All the angels were standing around the throne, the elders, and the four living creatures; and they fell on their faces before his throne, and worshiped God, saying, "Amen! Blessing, glory, wisdom, thanksgiving, honor, power, and might, be to our God forever and ever! Amen."

One of the elders answered, saying to me, "These who are arrayed in the white robes, who are they, and where did they come from?"

I told him, "My lord, you know."

He said to me, "These are those who came out of the great suffering. They washed their robes, and made them white in the Lamb's blood. Therefore they are before the throne of God, they serve him day and night in his temple. He who sits on the throne will spread his tabernacle over them. They will never be hungry or thirsty any more. The sun won't beat on them, nor any heat; for the Lamb who is in the middle of the throne shepherds them and leads them to springs of life-giving waters. And God will wipe away every tear from their eyes."

—Rev. 7:9–17

I saw a new heaven and a new earth: for the first heaven and the first earth have passed away, and the sea is no more. I saw the holy city, New Jerusalem, coming down out of heaven from God, prepared like a bride adorned for her husband. I heard a loud voice out of heaven saying, "Behold, God's dwelling is with people, and he will dwell with them, and they will be his people, and God himself will be with them as their God. He will wipe away every tear from their eyes. Death will be no more; neither will there be mourning, nor crying, nor pain, any more. The first things have passed away."

He who sits on the throne said, "Behold, I am making all things new." He said, "Write, for these words of God are faithful and true." He said to me, "I am the Alpha and the Omega, the Beginning and the End. I will give freely to him who is thirsty from the spring of the water of life. He who overcomes, I will give him these things. I will be his God, and he will be my son."

—Rev. 21:1–7

The twelve gates were twelve pearls. Each one of the gates was made of one pearl. The street of the city was pure gold, like transparent glass. I saw no temple in it, for the Lord God, the Almighty, and the Lamb, are its temple.

—Rev. 21:21–22

There will in no way enter into it anything profane, or one who causes an abomination or a lie, but only those who are written in the Lamb's book of life.

—Rev. 21:27

He showed me a river of water of life, clear as crystal, proceeding out of the throne of God and of the Lamb, in the middle of its street. On this side of the river and on that was the tree of life, bearing twelve kinds of fruits, yielding its fruit every month. The leaves of the tree were for the healing of the nations. There will be no curse any more. The throne of God and of the Lamb will be in it, and his servants will serve him. They will see his face, and his name will be on their foreheads. There will be no night, and they need no lamp light or sun light; for the Lord God will illuminate them. They will reign forever and ever.

—Rev. 22:1–5

Pray like this:
    "Our Father in heaven, may your name be kept holy.
    Let your Kingdom come.
     Let your will be done on earth as it is in heaven.
    Give us today our daily bread.
    Forgive us our debts,
     as we also forgive our debtors.
    Bring us not into temptation,
     but deliver us from the evil one.
    For yours is the Kingdom, the power, and the glory forever.
    Amen."

—Matt. 6:9–13

Besides praying *"your will be done,"* we have a responsibility to bring heaven to earth today.

This Good News of the Kingdom will be preached in the whole world for a testimony to all the nations, and then the end will come.

—Matt. 24:14

ARE YOU
A SANCTUARY?

As we sang the song "Sanctuary" by Randy Scruggs and John Thompson in church one Sunday, I pondered the meaning of the word *sanctuary*. I always thought that *sanctuary*, *tabernacle*, and *temple* were synonyms. Here's what Exodus says:

> *You will bring them in, and plant them in the mountain of your inheritance, the place, Yahweh, which you have made for yourself to dwell in; the sanctuary, Lord, which your hands have established.*
>
> —Exod. 15:17

> *Then the cloud covered the Tent of Meeting, and Yahweh's glory filled the tabernacle. Moses wasn't able to enter into the Tent of Meeting, because the cloud stayed on it, and Yahweh's glory filled the tabernacle.*
>
> —Exod. 40:34–35

Based on the common church use of the word, the song implies that we should be made a place for God to dwell. There are multiple scriptures that support this idea.

> *Or don't you know that your body is a temple of the Holy Spirit who is in you, whom you have from God? You are not*

your own, for you were bought with a price. Therefore glorify God in your body and in your spirit, which are God's.

—1 Cor. 6:19–20

Don't you know that you are a temple of God, and that God's Spirit lives in you? If anyone destroys God's temple, God will destroy him; for God's temple is holy, which you are.

—1 Cor. 3:16–17

What agreement does a temple of God have with idols? For you are a temple of the living God. Even as God said, "I will dwell in them and walk in them. I will be their God and they will be my people."

—2 Cor. 6:16

But you are not in the flesh but in the Spirit, if it is so that the Spirit of God dwells in you. But if any man doesn't have the Spirit of Christ, he is not his.

—Rom. 8:9

Jesus answered him, "If a man loves me, he will keep my word. My Father will love him, and we will come to him, and make our home with him."

—John 14:23

But Christ is faithful as a Son over his house. We are his house, if we hold fast our confidence and the glorying of our hope firm to the end.

—Heb. 3:6

So then you are no longer strangers and foreigners, but you are fellow citizens with the saints and of the household of God, being built on the foundation of the apostles and prophets, Christ Jesus himself being the chief cornerstone; in whom the whole building, fitted together, grows into a holy temple in the Lord; in whom you also are built together for a habitation of God in the Spirit.

—Eph. 2:19–22

But God's dwelling in us is just a beginning. We must also worship and praise God with prayer and thanksgiving from our hearts.

Therefore I urge you, brothers, by the mercies of God, to present your bodies a living sacrifice, holy, acceptable to God, which is your spiritual service.

—Rom. 12:1

I will bring these to my holy mountain,
  and make them joyful in my house of prayer.
Their burnt offerings and their sacrifices will be accepted on my altar;
  for my house will be called a house of prayer for all peoples.

—Isa. 56:7

Coming to him, a living stone, rejected indeed by men, but chosen by God, precious. You also, as living stones, are built up as a spiritual house, to be a holy priesthood, to offer up spiritual sacrifices, acceptable to God through Jesus Christ.

—1 Pet. 2:4–5

I was satisfied with my understanding of *sanctuary*. My praise and worship were probably not demonstrative enough, but I was content. Then God said to me, "You're missing half the point." Sanctuary has a second meaning, which was a revelation for me. Here is how the *Merriam-Webster* online dictionary defines it:

A consecrated place: such as: the ancient Hebrew temple at Jerusalem or its holy of holies; the most sacred part of a religious building (such as the part of a Christian church in which the altar is placed); the room in which general worship services are held; a place (such as a church or a temple) for worship; a place of refuge and protection; a refuge for wildlife where predators are controlled and hunting is illegal; the immunity from law attached to a sanctuary.

Yes, we must open our hearts to God, offer him a place inside us, and have him occupy our being. But his occupancy should change us. We should be a sanctuary for others—a refuge, a place of comfort, confidence, and strength. I can't say what the composers thought as they wrote the song "Sanctuary," but for me it became an invitation for God to make me a refuge of protection from predators (Satan). Take power from these verses:

Blessed be the God and Father of our Lord Jesus Christ, the Father of mercies and God of all comfort; who comforts us in all our affliction, that we may be able to comfort those who are in any affliction, through the comfort with which we ourselves are comforted by God.

—2 Cor. 1:3–4

He has said to me, "My grace is sufficient for you, for my power is made perfect in weakness." Most gladly therefore I will rather glory in my weaknesses, that the power of Christ may rest on me.

—2 Cor. 12:9

Peace I leave with you. My peace I give to you; not as the world gives, I give to you. Don't let your heart be troubled, neither let it be fearful.

—John 14:27

Don't you be afraid, for I am with you.
  Don't be dismayed, for I am your God.
  I will strengthen you.
  Yes, I will help you.
  Yes, I will uphold you with the right hand of my righteousness.
                                                        —Isa. 41:10

I have told you these things, that in me you may have peace. In the world you have trouble; but cheer up! I have overcome the world.
                                                        —John 16:33

What then shall we say about these things? If God is for us, who can be against us?
                                                        —Rom. 8:31

Be strong and courageous. Don't be afraid or scared of them; for Yahweh your God himself is who goes with you. He will not fail you nor forsake you.
                                                        —Deut. 31:6

Trust in Yahweh with all your heart,
  and don't lean on your own understanding.
In all your ways acknowledge him,
  and he will make your paths straight.
                                                        —Prov. 3:5–6

This is the boldness which we have toward him, that if we ask anything according to his will, he listens to us.
                                                        —1 John 5:14

Therefore, my beloved brothers, be steadfast, immovable, always abounding in the Lord's work, because you know that your labor is not in vain in the Lord.
                                                        —1 Cor. 15:58

My flesh and my heart fails,
*   but God is the strength of my heart and my portion forever.*
                                                        —Ps. 73:26

But the Lord is faithful, who will establish you and guard you
from the evil one.
                                                        —2 Thess. 3:3

Yahweh is my strength and my shield.
*   My heart has trusted in him, and I am helped.*
Therefore my heart greatly rejoices.
*   With my song I will thank him.*
                                                        —Ps. 28:7

How does God prepare us to be a sanctuary, not only a place where he dwells and we worship and praise him, but also a place of refuge to a lost world?

Seek Yahweh and his strength.
*   Seek his face forever more.*
                                                        —1 Chron. 16:11

Don't be conformed to this world, but be transformed by the
renewing of your mind, so that you may prove what is the
good, well-pleasing, and perfect will of God.
                                                        —Rom. 12:2

Jesus answered, "The greatest is, 'Hear, Israel, the Lord our
God, the Lord is one: you shall love the Lord your God with
all your heart, and with all your soul, and with all your mind,
and with all your strength.' This is the first commandment."
                                                        —Mark 12:29–30

If Christians don't create a place of sanctuary, a refuge, from the crazy world, who will?

❖

WITH
A PURPOSE

We often celebrate Independence Day with patriotic songs such as "Battle Hymn of the Republic." The last line of the last verse sticks out to me. It has been modified from the original. Here is the original with my emphasis added:

> In the beauty of the lilies Christ was born across the sea,
> With a glory in His bosom that transfigures you and me;
> As He died to make men holy, let us *die* to make men free,
> While God is marching on (emphasis added).[3]

Here is the modified version as sung by Fred Waring and the Pennsylvanians in the 1940s and early 1950s:

> In the beauty of the lilies Christ was born across the sea,
> With a glory in His bosom that transfigures you and me;
> As He died to make men holy, let us *live* to make men free!
> While God is marching on (emphasis added).[4]

---

3. Julia Ward Howe, "The Battle Hymn of the Republic," *The Atlantic*, February 1862.
4. Julia Ward Howe, "Battle Hymn of the Republic," performed by Fred Waring and the Pennsylvanians, *YouTube*, https://www.youtube.com/watch?v=zDM7X2tjcKo.

I like the modification. What does it mean for us to live as Christ died? That question begs this follow-up question: How did Christ die? I don't mean his crucifixion but rather the story behind the crucifixion. Is there a lesson for us?

Jesus had a purpose for coming to earth, a purpose clearly defined in John 3:16: *"For God so loved the world, that he gave his one and only Son, that whoever believes in him should not perish, but have eternal life."* Jesus always understood his purpose.

> *When he was twelve years old, they went up to Jerusalem according to the custom of the feast, and when they had fulfilled the days, as they were returning, the boy Jesus stayed behind in Jerusalem. Joseph and his mother didn't know it, but supposing him to be in the company, they went a day's journey, and they looked for him among their relatives and acquaintances. When they didn't find him, they returned to Jerusalem, looking for him. After three days they found him in the temple, sitting in the middle of the teachers, both listening to them, and asking them questions. All who heard him were amazed at his understanding and his answers. When they saw him, they were astonished, and his mother said to him, "Son, why have you treated us this way? Behold, your father and I were anxiously looking for you."*
>
> *He said to them, "Why were you looking for me? Didn't you know that I must be in my Father's house?" They didn't understand the saying which he spoke to them.*
>
> —Luke 2:42–50

Jesus taught many lessons, forgave many sins, and healed many people during his ministry. He taught with a purpose.

> *Don't think that I came to send peace on the earth. I didn't come to send peace, but a sword.*
>
> —Matt. 10:34

The world can't hate you, but it hates me, because I testify about it, that its works are evil.

—John 7:7

Jesus said to them, "I am the bread of life. Whoever comes to me will not be hungry, and whoever believes in me will never be thirsty. But I told you that you have seen me, and yet you don't believe. All those whom the Father gives me will come to me. He who comes to me I will in no way throw out. For I have come down from heaven, not to do my own will, but the will of him who sent me. This is the will of my Father who sent me, that of all he has given to me I should lose nothing, but should raise him up at the last day. This is the will of the one who sent me, that everyone who sees the Son, and believes in him, should have eternal life; and I will raise him up at the last day."

—John 6:35–40

He also prepared those around him for what was to come.

From that time, Jesus began to show his disciples that he must go to Jerusalem and suffer many things from the elders, chief priests, and scribes, and be killed, and the third day be raised up.

—Matt. 16:21

The Son of Man must suffer many things, and be rejected by the elders, chief priests, and scribes, and be killed, and the third day be raised up.

—Luke 9:22

He said to them, "Foolish men, and slow of heart to believe in all that the prophets have spoken! Didn't the Christ have to suffer these things and to enter into his glory?"

—Luke 24:25–26

He said to them, "Thus it is written, and thus it was necessary for the Christ to suffer and to rise from the dead the third day."
—Luke 24:46

He said to them, "I have earnestly desired to eat this Passover with you before I suffer."
—Luke 22:15

So how did Jesus die? He died as he lived—with a purpose. He knew his purpose well and what he had to do to achieve that purpose. And he charged full speed ahead toward that purpose. "As he died to make men holy, let us live to make men free." How do we live to make men free? With a purpose—a purpose to make them free.

But what is free?

There are several verses that help us understand what God means when he calls us to be free.

> *Jesus therefore said to those Jews who had believed him, "If you remain in my word, then you are truly my disciples. You will know the truth, and the truth will make you free."*
>
> *They answered him, "We are Abraham's offspring, and have never been in bondage to anyone. How do you say, 'You will be made free'?"*
>
> *Jesus answered them, "Most certainly I tell you, everyone who commits sin is the bondservant of sin. A bondservant doesn't live in the house forever. A son remains forever. If therefore the Son makes you free, you will be free indeed."*
> —John 8:31–36

The Spirit of the Lord is on me,
because he has anointed me to preach good news to the poor.
He has sent me to heal the broken hearted,
  to proclaim release to the captives,
  recovering of sight to the blind,
  to deliver those who are crushed.
—Luke 4:18

Now the Lord is the Spirit and where the Spirit of the Lord is, there is liberty.

—2 Cor. 3:17

But now, being made free from sin and having become servants of God, you have your fruit of sanctification and the result of eternal life.

—Rom. 6:22

There is therefore now no condemnation to those who are in Christ Jesus, who don't walk according to the flesh, but according to the Spirit. For the law of the Spirit of life in Christ Jesus made me free from the law of sin and of death. For what the law couldn't do, in that it was weak through the flesh, God did, sending his own Son in the likeness of sinful flesh and for sin, he condemned sin in the flesh; that the ordinance of the law might be fulfilled in us, who walk not after the flesh, but after the Spirit.

—Rom. 8:1–4

I will walk in liberty,
*   for I have sought your precepts.*

—Ps. 119:45

But he who looks into the perfect law of freedom and continues, not being a hearer who forgets, but a doer of the work, this man will be blessed in what he does.

—James 1:25

Freedom is knowing Jesus as our Lord and Savior and doing our best to follow his commandments. Therefore, it follows that living to make men free is living to share the gospel.

So faith comes by hearing, and hearing by the word of God.

—Rom. 10:17

Jesus therefore said to them again, "Peace be to you. As the Father has sent me, even so I send you."

—John 20:21

Jesus came to them and spoke to them, saying, "All authority has been given to me in heaven and on earth. Go and make disciples of all nations, baptizing them in the name of the Father and of the Son and of the Holy Spirit, teaching them to observe all things that I commanded you. Behold, I am with you always, even to the end of the age." Amen.

—Matt. 28:18–20

Purpose is different from destiny. Destiny implies that we have no say, that the outcome is automatic. Jesus lived with and died with a purpose based on his own decision to do so. For us to live with a purpose, we must decide to do so as well. We have no automatic purpose; we have to accept Jesus as our Savior and make him our Lord. We then have to allow his lordship to make a difference in our life, to give us direction and purpose. Our purpose will not always be easy, but again, "as He died to make men holy, let us live to make men free!"

Jesus answered them, "The time has come for the Son of Man to be glorified. Most certainly I tell you, unless a grain of wheat falls into the earth and dies, it remains by itself alone. But if it dies, it bears much fruit. He who loves his life will lose it. He who hates his life in this world will keep it to eternal life. If anyone serves me, let him follow me. Where I am, there my servant will also be. If anyone serves me, the Father will honor him.

"Now my soul is troubled. What shall I say? 'Father, save me from this time?' But I came to this time for this cause. Father, glorify your name!"

Then a voice came out of the sky, saying, "I have both glorified it, and will glorify it again."

—John 12:23–28

If the world hates you, you know that it has hated me before it hated you. If you were of the world, the world would love its own. But because you are not of the world, since I chose you out of the world, therefore the world hates you. Remember the word that I said to you: "A servant is not greater than his lord." If they persecuted me, they will also persecute you. If they kept my word, they will also keep yours.

—John 15:18–20

Fortunately, if we are looking to Jesus, we see the end in sight.

Looking to Jesus, the author and perfecter of faith, who for the joy that was set before him endured the cross, despising its shame, and has sat down at the right hand of the throne of God.

—Heb. 12:2

If I go and prepare a place for you, I will come again, and will receive you to myself; that where I am, you may be there also.

—John 14:3

Now that is living with a purpose!

❖

INFLUENCE

The Pharisees and Sadducees came, and testing him, asked him to show them a sign from heaven. But he answered them, "When it is evening, you say, 'It will be fair weather, for the sky is red.' In the morning, 'It will be foul weather today, for the sky is red and threatening.' Hypocrites! You know how to discern the appearance of the sky, but you can't discern the signs of the times! An evil and adulterous generation seeks after a sign, and there will be no sign given to it, except the sign of the prophet Jonah."

He left them and departed. The disciples came to the other side and had forgotten to take bread. Jesus said to them, "Take heed and beware of the yeast of the Pharisees and Sadducees."

They reasoned among themselves, saying, "We brought no bread."

Jesus, perceiving it, said, "Why do you reason among yourselves, you of little faith, because you have brought no bread? Don't you yet perceive or remember the five loaves for the five thousand, and how many baskets you took up, or the seven loaves for the four thousand, and how many baskets you took up? How is it that you don't perceive that I didn't speak to you concerning bread? But beware of the yeast of the Pharisees and Sadducees."

Then they understood that he didn't tell them to beware of the yeast of bread, but of the teaching of the Pharisees and Sadducees.

*Now when Jesus came into the parts of Caesarea Philippi,
he asked his disciples, saying, "Who do men say that I, the Son
of Man, am?"*

*They said, "Some say John the Baptizer, some, Elijah, and
others, Jeremiah or one of the prophets."*

He said to them, "But who do you say that I am?"

*Simon Peter answered, "You are the Christ, the Son of the
living God."*

*Jesus answered him, "Blessed are you, Simon Bar Jonah,
for flesh and blood has not revealed this to you, but my Father
who is in heaven. I also tell you that you are Peter, and on this
rock I will build my assembly, and the gates of Hades will not
prevail against it."*

—Matt. 16:1–18

The Holy Scriptures remain new, fresh, informative, and instructional. There are great lessons here that speak to us today. In the first section, the Pharisees and Sadducees ask Jesus for a sign. Jesus tells them that while they think they need a special sign, in reality, they are missing the signs all around them. That the skies are predictable, that there are seasons, that all forms of life can reproduce—these things should have been a sign to them just as much as the miracles he performed.

We should see signs and miracles all around us every day. If we don't, we're missing God, or at least taking him for granted. People say, "I'm sick and tired of_____." My response is this: *"Take heed and beware of the yeast"* of the world. What is yeast and what does it do? Yeast is actually a fungus. It creates gas bubbles that eventually burst, leaving air pockets in bread dough. In other words, yeast is an influencer that leaves nothing behind when it's done. And it takes very little yeast to get large results.

*Your boasting is not good. Don't you know that a little yeast
leavens the whole lump?*

—1 Cor. 5:6

Our minds today are constantly bombarded with garbage. From radio, television, 24-hour news, and social media, our minds are constantly filled. Jesus's caution applies to us: *"Take heed and beware of the yeast."* Beware of the influence the world and culture have on you. It takes only a little to make a large impact. My wife often says, "Be careful little ears what you hear, be careful little eyes what you see." And, as I've said before, be careful what you say. Your own voice is the greatest influencer you have.

In the second section of the passage from Matthew 16, Jesus asks his disciples who others say that he is. They tell him that many think he is a famous prophet come back to life. Peter said, *"You are the Christ."* Jesus responded, *"On this rock I will build my assembly."* There are many interpretations of this verse. Some say Peter is the rock Jesus refers to. Some say Peter's confession—the same one we all make when we make Jesus the Lord of our lives—is the rock. I understand why some believe that Peter himself is the rock, but I think that interpretation conflicts with other scriptures (one written by Peter) that list Jesus as the cornerstone.

> *Coming to him, a living stone, rejected indeed by men, but chosen by God, precious. You also, as living stones, are built up as a spiritual house, to be a holy priesthood, to offer up spiritual sacrifices, acceptable to God through Jesus Christ. Because it is contained in Scripture,*
>
> > *"Behold, I lay in Zion a chief cornerstone, chosen and precious: He who believes in him will not be disappointed."*
>
> *For you who believe therefore is the honor, but for those who are disobedient,*
>
> > *"The stone which the builders rejected has become the chief cornerstone,"*
>
> *and,*
>
> > *"a stumbling stone and a rock of offense."*
>
> —1 Pet. 2:4–8

I also understand the second interpretation of the confession of faith as the rock. But I think the answer is one step back from that. Look at the previous verse (Matt. 16:17): *"For flesh and blood has not revealed this to you, but my Father who is in heaven."* It seems that the personal revelation from God to each of us—the voice that leads us to accept Jesus—is the true rock on which Jesus would build the church. Consider John 6:44: *"No one can come to me unless the Father who sent me draws him, and I will raise him up in the last day."* It is God's influence on each of us through his Son, his Word, and the Holy Spirit on which the great works of the church are based.

God wants to be the influence in our lives. *"For this is good and acceptable in the sight of God our Savior, who desires all people to be saved and come to full knowledge of the truth"* (1 Tim. 2:3–4). Creation bears constant witness to God. Jesus warned the disciples of bad influences. Upon God's influence on our lives, he will build his church. Who or what influences you? Take time to review what influence the world has on your thoughts, actions, feelings, and attitudes.

> *Don't be conformed to this world, but be transformed by the renewing of your mind, so that you may prove what is the good, well-pleasing, and perfect will of God.*
>
> —Rom. 12:2

TRUST

Behold, one came to him and said, "Good teacher, what good thing shall I do, that I may have eternal life?"

He said to him, "Why do you call me good? No one is good but one, that is, God. But if you want to enter into life, keep the commandments."

He said to him, "Which ones?"

Jesus said, "'You shall not murder.' 'You shall not commit adultery.' 'You shall not steal.' 'You shall not offer false testimony.' 'Honor your father and your mother.' And, 'You shall love your neighbor as yourself.'"

The young man said to him, "All these things I have observed from my youth. What do I still lack?"

Jesus said to him, "If you want to be perfect, go, sell what you have, and give to the poor, and you will have treasure in heaven; and come, follow me." But when the young man heard this, he went away sad, for he was one who had great possessions.

Jesus said to his disciples, "Most certainly I say to you, a rich man will enter into the Kingdom of Heaven with difficulty. Again I tell you, it is easier for a camel to go through a needle's eye than for a rich man to enter into God's Kingdom."

When the disciples heard it, they were exceedingly astonished, saying, "Who then can be saved?"

Looking at them, Jesus said, "With men this is impossible, but with God all things are possible."

—Matt. 19:16–26

As with earlier verses from Matthew, our traditional assumptions about them don't reflect their full meaning. The first assumption is that because Jesus said *"keep the commandments,"* we can earn our place in heaven, but we know we cannot earn salvation. The Old Testament law was never a path to God but a mirror for us to look into and see that we can never be good enough to keep *all* the law. Jesus didn't tell the rich young man to follow the law because it would get him to heaven; he told him to follow the law to show him that he wasn't perfect, that he couldn't *do* anything to earn eternal life. But, like many of us, the young man considered himself a fairly righteous man who had kept all the laws and had therefore missed the point. He did not deserve heaven and could not earn it. If we think we can earn heaven by our works, we have missed the point as well.

For by grace you have been saved through faith, and that not of yourselves; it is the gift of God, not of works, that no one would boast.

—Eph. 2:8–9

The second common assumption is that by giving away all we have and becoming poor, we will earn God's approval. Jesus told the rich young ruler to sell all he had, give it to the poor, and follow him. Again, Jesus didn't tell the young man to do so simply to earn heaven; he did so to show the young man his weakness. The young man clearly enjoyed and perhaps relied on his possessions. Therefore, he left Jesus, dejected, having once again missed the point.

Jesus then said that it is difficult for a rich man to enter heaven; indeed, it is easier for a camel to go through the eye of a needle. By the world's standards, Americans in the United States are rich. Such standards suggest it is difficult for any of us to make it into heaven. Because of that, many suggest the eye of a needle was a small gate in the city wall that required a camel to get down on its belly and crawl in order to get through—extremely difficult for the camel but not impossible. We like this theory because it allows the possibility for the rich to get into heaven. We want to believe that *we* can do it. I believe that Jesus was talking about the literal eye of a sewing needle. If so, it is clearly impossible for the rich to make it to heaven—on their own, that is.

The real question for both the rich ruler and for us today is this: Whom do you trust? The young ruler trusted in himself and his riches. He was confident in his ability to be good enough. He trusted in his possessions more than he trusted in Jesus. Similarly, if we are looking for a loophole such as a small wall gate, we are trusting in ourselves and our own abilities. I don't know about you, but I make too many mistakes to trust myself to get to heaven!

> *Because by the works of the law, no flesh will be justified in his sight; for through the law comes the knowledge of sin.*
>
> *But now apart from the law, a righteousness of God has been revealed, being testified by the law and the prophets; even the righteousness of God through faith in Jesus Christ to all and on all those who believe. For there is no distinction, for all have sinned, and fall short of the glory of God.*
>
> —Rom. 3:20–23

But there is one more sentence: *"With men this is impossible, but with God all things are possible"* (Matt. 19:26).

> *The fear of man proves to be a snare,*
> *but whoever puts his trust in Yahweh is kept safe.*
> —Prov. 29:25

> *Those who know your name will put their trust in you,*
> *for you, Yahweh, have not forsaken those who seek you.*
> —Ps. 9:10

Behold, God is my salvation. I will trust, and will not be afraid; for Yah, Yahweh, is my strength and song; and he has become my salvation.

—Isa. 12:2

Blessed is the man who trusts in Yahweh,
  and whose confidence is in Yahweh.
For he will be as a tree planted by the waters,
  who spreads out its roots by the river,
and will not fear when heat comes,
  but its leaf will be green,
and will not be concerned in the year of drought.
  It won't cease from yielding fruit.

—Jer. 17:7–8

In nothing be anxious, but in everything, by prayer and petition with thanksgiving, let your requests be made known to God. And the peace of God, which surpasses all understanding, will guard your hearts and your thoughts in Christ Jesus.

—Phil. 4:6–7

Therefore I tell you, don't be anxious for your life: what you will eat, or what you will drink; nor yet for your body, what you will wear. Isn't life more than food, and the body more than clothing? See the birds of the sky, that they don't sow, neither do they reap, nor gather into barns. Your heavenly Father feeds them. Aren't you of much more value than they?

—Matt. 6:25–26

We know that all things work together for good for those who love God, for those who are called according to his purpose.

—Rom. 8:28

Commit your way to Yahweh.
    Trust also in him, and he will do this.

—Ps. 37:5

My God will supply every need of yours according to his riches
in glory in Christ Jesus.

—Phil. 4:19

Trust in Yahweh with all your heart,
    and don't lean on your own understanding.
In all your ways acknowledge him,
    and he will make your paths straight.

—Prov. 3:5–6

The Bible is full of God's message: Trust me. Noah, Abraham, Moses, Joshua, David, Shadrach, Meshach, Abednego, Daniel, Elijah, Mary, Joseph, the disciples, and Paul are just a few examples of those who trusted God for direction, comfort, protection, and provision. The end of God's Word says, *"He who testifies these things says, 'Yes, I come quickly.' Amen! Yes, come, Lord Jesus"* (Rev. 22:20).

In this time, in this season, whom do you trust?

---◆---

PATIENT
BUT PREPARED

Jesus went out from the temple, and was going on his way. His disciples came to him to show him the buildings of the temple. But he answered them, "You see all of these things, don't you? Most certainly I tell you, there will not be left here one stone on another, that will not be thrown down."

As he sat on the Mount of Olives, the disciples came to him privately, saying, "Tell us, when will these things be? What is the sign of your coming, and of the end of the age?"

Jesus answered them, "Be careful that no one leads you astray. For many will come in my name, saying, 'I am the Christ,' and will lead many astray. You will hear of wars and rumors of wars. See that you aren't troubled, for all this must happen, but the end is not yet. For nation will rise against nation, and kingdom against kingdom; and there will be famines, plagues, and earthquakes in various places. But all these things are the beginning of birth pains.

"Then they will deliver you up to oppression and will kill you. You will be hated by all of the nations for my name's sake. Then many will stumble, and will deliver up one another, and will hate one another. Many false prophets will arise and will lead many astray. Because iniquity will be multiplied, the love of many will grow cold. But he who endures to the end will be

saved. This Good News of the Kingdom will be preached in the whole world for a testimony to all the nations, and then the end will come."

—Matt. 24:1–14

(See also Mark 13 and Luke 21:5–38)

Matthew 24 details Jesus's final week before his crucifixion. He has already made his final entrance into the city of Jerusalem and has just held several conversations with the Pharisees, Sadducees, and Herodians— all who were trying to trap him with his words. Of course, Jesus, in full wisdom of the Father, not only avoided their traps but also taught them the true meaning of the Word.

Then Jesus left the temple for the final time. I wonder if the conversations impacted his temperament—possibly made him angry, frustrated, tired, or even invigorated—for it seems as if the disciples tried to distract him by pointing out the beauty of the temple. Unimpressed by the beauty of the man-made buildings, Jesus said they would soon be rubble. Remember, beauty is only temporary. Find beauty beyond what the naked eye beholds. *"While we don't look at the things which are seen, but at the things which are not seen. For the things which are seen are temporal, but the things which are not seen are eternal"* (2 Cor. 4:18).

The disciples then asked when the destruction would happen, when Jesus would return, and when the end of the age would occur, assuming all were related. Jesus's answers imply the need for patience. We must wait and not fall prey to deception. Then and now, men have claimed to be the Messiah. *"Little children, these are the end times, and as you heard that the Antichrist is coming, even now many antichrists have arisen. By this we know that it is the final hour"* (1 John 2:18). *"Do not be led astray"* also means do not be led astray by wrong doctrine. That many could be deceived proves that many do not know scripture well. Know who Jesus is and how to recognize him when he does return. You know him through his Word, so read and study every day. *"You will know the truth, and the truth will make you free"* (John 8:32). Jesus said that for those who are paying attention, his return will be obvious. *"For as the lightning flashes from the east, and is seen even to the west, so will the coming of the Son of Man be"* (Matt. 24:27).

Next, Jesus spoke of wars and rumors of wars, as well as nation against nation, kingdom against kingdom (some interpret this as race against race), earthquakes, famines, and pestilence. Many look at our times and declare, "The end is near! Jesus will soon return!" But history shows us that our struggles have been present since Jesus spoke these words. Why the declarations? Commentators suggest that each generation needs to feel the urgency of Jesus's return. We want to be rescued from our times rather than fight the good fight. As we have seen in the United States over the last 50 years, it is easy to become complacent.

> *For this people's heart has grown callous,*
>> *their ears are dull of hearing,*
>> *and they have closed their eyes;*
> *or else perhaps they might perceive with their eyes,*
>> *hear with their ears,*
>> *understand with their heart,*
> *and would turn again,*
>> *and I would heal them.*
>
> —Matt. 13:15

There is a danger in proclaiming the end times in terms of anything other than the broad terms described here. In fact, Jesus says later in Matthew that *"no one knows of that day and hour, not even the angels of heaven, but my Father only"* (Matt. 24:36). Too many people have put their faith in an end-times prediction only to see the predicted time come and go. Too many then walk away from faith, wondering what and whom they can trust.

Jesus concluded, *"But all these things are the beginning of birth pains."* I have no experience with birth pains, but I know that birth pains generally increase in frequency and intensity as the grand event draws closer. In other words, the signs are only the beginning; there will be more to come, and it will likely get worse before it gets better.

He then told them of persecution and death for his sake. Of course, he was warning them of their own future, but I think Jesus was also giving us an expectation. Faith in God's Word today can earn a person all sorts of descriptors and, in parts of the world, even death. But these and other verses tell us to expect and endure it all.

> *Beloved, don't be astonished at the fiery trial which has come upon you to test you, as though a strange thing happened to you.*
> —1 Pet. 4:12

> *They overcame him because of the Lamb's blood, and because of the word of their testimony. They didn't love their life, even to death.*
> —Rev. 12:11

Many will stumble and fall away. They will not be willing to be persecuted for Christ's sake because of whom they trust and what they allow to influence them. We desire to be part of the world more than we desire to stand for Jesus. Many have fallen away from the truth and forgotten the good news of Jesus, opting instead for the false security of the world they know. *"Don't be deceived! Evil companionships corrupt good morals"* (1 Cor. 15:33).

Be prepared intellectually and emotionally to stand for Christ.

> *Don't be unequally yoked with unbelievers, for what fellowship do righteousness and iniquity have? Or what fellowship does light have with darkness? What agreement does Christ have with Belial? Or what portion does a believer have with an unbeliever? What agreement does a temple of God have with idols? For you are a temple of the living God. Even as God said, "I will dwell in them and walk in them. I will be their God and they will be my people."*
> —2 Cor. 6:14–16

How do we prepare intellectually and emotionally?

Put on the whole armor of God, that you may be able to stand against the wiles of the devil. For our wrestling is not against flesh and blood, but against the principalities, against the powers, against the world's rulers of the darkness of this age, and against the spiritual forces of wickedness in the heavenly places. Therefore put on the whole armor of God, that you may be able to withstand in the evil day, and having done all, to stand. Stand therefore, having the utility belt of truth buckled around your waist, and having put on the breastplate of righteousness, and having fitted your feet with the preparation of the Good News of peace, above all, taking up the shield of faith, with which you will be able to quench all the fiery darts of the evil one. And take the helmet of salvation, and the sword of the Spirit, which is the word of God; with all prayer and requests, praying at all times in the Spirit, and being watchful to this end in all perseverance and requests for all the saints.

—Eph. 6:11–18

Jesus then announced the final and most challenging event to hasten his coming. *"This Good News of the Kingdom will be preached in the whole world for a testimony to all the nations, and then the end will come"* (Matt. 24:14). Many argue that the gospel has reached the whole world, for the Holy Bible is available around the world right now. While that is probably true, are people really hearing the good news? The good news is that Jesus died for us and that we must accept his salvation and invite him into our hearts, which will make us strive to keep his commandments. *"Make my joy full by being like-minded, having the same love, being of one accord, of one mind; doing nothing through rivalry or through conceit, but in humility, each counting others better than himself; each of you not just looking to his own things, but each of you also to the things of others"* (Phil. 2:2–4). There are still people who believe they must earn their way to heaven. They still need to hear the good news that they can't, but Jesus already has!

It is our job to explain the difference between following the law and accepting the gift of salvation through Jesus.

> *Brothers, my heart's desire and my prayer to God is for Israel, that they may be saved. For I testify about them that they have a zeal for God, but not according to knowledge. For being ignorant of God's righteousness, and seeking to establish their own righteousness, they didn't subject themselves to the righteousness of God. For Christ is the fulfillment of the law for righteousness to everyone who believes. For Moses writes about the righteousness of the law, "The one who does them will live by them." But the righteousness which is of faith says this, "Don't say in your heart, 'Who will ascend into heaven?' (that is, to bring Christ down); or, 'Who will descend into the abyss?' (that is, to bring Christ up from the dead.)" But what does it say? "The word is near you, in your mouth, and in your heart;" that is, the word of faith which we preach: that if you will confess with your mouth that Jesus is Lord, and believe in your heart that God raised him from the dead, you will be saved. For with the heart, one believes resulting in righteousness; and with the mouth confession is made resulting in salvation. For the Scripture says, "Whoever believes in him will not be disappointed."*
>
> *For there is no distinction between Jew and Greek; for the same Lord is Lord of all, and is rich to all who call on him. For, "Whoever will call on the name of the Lord will be saved."*
>
> —Rom. 10:1–13

We don't know the timing of the last day, but we should be patient and prepared for that day. And it will be a glorious day!

He showed me a river of water of life, clear as crystal, proceeding out of the throne of God and of the Lamb, in the middle of its street. On this side of the river and on that was the tree of life, bearing twelve kinds of fruits, yielding its fruit every month. The leaves of the tree were for the healing of the nations. There will be no curse any more. The throne of God and of the Lamb will be in it, and his servants will serve him. They will see his face, and his name will be on their foreheads. There will be no night, and they need no lamp light or sun light; for the Lord God will illuminate them. They will reign forever and ever.

—Rev. 22:1–5

Amen!

WHY

CHRISTIANITY?

The world today seems to minimize the importance of living a Christ-centered life and having a Christ-centered point of view. So what is Christianity, and what makes it different from the world's religions? In simple terms, it is a relationship, it is already done, and it is true.

Christianity is not a religion, despite what the dictionary says. Let's look at the definition of religion according to the *Merriam-Webster* online dictionary: "The service and worship of God or the supernatural; commitment or devotion to religious faith or observance; a personal set or institutionalized system of religious attitudes, beliefs, and practices; scrupulous conformity; a cause, principle, or system of beliefs held to with ardor and faith." The dictionary defines Christianity as "the religion derived from Jesus Christ, based on the Bible as sacred scripture." Yes, Christianity is derived from Jesus as the Christ and is certainly based on the Holy Bible as sacred scripture, but it is so much more than worship, devotion, beliefs, and principles.

Christianity is all about relationship. God doesn't seek our service, worship, or devotion. He seeks a personal relationship with each of us. Of course, that relationship will naturally lead us to service, worship, thanksgiving, devotion, and so forth, but it's the relationship that God desires. How do we know that? Before he created human beings, he had angels to worship him. But he made people in his own image—for relationship.

In the beginning was the Word, and the Word was with God, and the Word was God. The same was in the beginning with God. All things were made through him. Without him, nothing was made that has been made. In him was life, and the life was the light of men. The light shines in the darkness, and the darkness hasn't overcome it.

—John 1:1–5

For God so loved the world, that he gave his one and only Son, that whoever believes in him should not perish, but have eternal life. For God didn't send his Son into the world to judge the world, but that the world should be saved through him.

—John 3:16–17

The Word became flesh, and lived among us. We saw his glory, such glory as of the one and only Son of the Father, full of grace and truth.

—John 1:14

No one has seen God at any time. The one and only Son, who is in the bosom of the Father, has declared him.

—John 1:18

I and the Father are one.

—John 10:30

Certainly, Jesus was with God from the very beginning. He came to earth as one of us and showed us what a relationship with the Father should be. But he went even further than that. He wants that relationship to last for eternity, for we could never have eternity with him on our own.

For whoever keeps the whole law, and yet stumbles in one point, he has become guilty of all.

—James 2:10

For all have sinned, and fall short of the glory of God.

—Rom. 3:23

Jesus not only came to earth and showed us the example of relationship with the Father, but he also bore all our transgressions: *"For him who knew no sin he made to be sin on our behalf; so that in him we might become the righteousness of God"* (2 Cor. 5:21). Think about that for a minute. We often take for granted what that means. He came to earth, showed us relationship, and then made that relationship with the Father possible. There is now a direct pathway for us to have a relationship with God.

Jesus said to him, "I am the way, the truth, and the life. No one comes to the Father, except through me."

—John 14:6

But God commends his own love toward us, in that while we were yet sinners, Christ died for us.
Much more then, being now justified by his blood, we will be saved from God's wrath through him. For if while we were enemies, we were reconciled to God through the death of his Son, much more, being reconciled, we will be saved by his life.

—Rom. 5:8–10

There is salvation in no one else, for there is no other name under heaven that is given among men, by which we must be saved!

—Acts 4:12

And it's already done. Christianity is founded in what Jesus did for us, not what we can do for him.

Without controversy, the mystery of godliness is great:
God was revealed in the flesh,
justified in the spirit,
seen by angels,
preached among the nations,
believed on in the world,
and received up in glory.

—1 Tim. 3:16

When I saw him, I fell at his feet like a dead man.
He laid his right hand on me, saying, "Don't be afraid. I
am the first and the last, and the Living one. I was dead, and
behold, I am alive forever and ever. Amen. I have the keys of
Death and of Hades."

—Rev. 1:17–18

In most world religions, believers must complete a set of tasks to gain a reward or meet a standard to be accepted by their god. But God knew we could never meet his standard, and we do fall short. Falling short in one area is the same as falling short in all areas. Fortunately, our eternity is not based on our performance but on Jesus's. *"Jesus said to her, 'I am the resurrection and the life. He who believes in me will still live, even if he dies. Whoever lives and believes in me will never die. Do you believe this?'"* (John 11:25–26). We have a Savior! We don't have to work to save ourselves. Our requirement is to humble ourselves, believe in his power, and recognize him as God's Son and our Savior.

And it's all true. Christianity is founded in God's inspired Word, the Holy Bible. As stated in John 1, the Word is Jesus, and the Holy Bible represents him. In the Old Testament, God established a relationship with his people through multiple encounters and revealed his perfect love through a Savior yet to come. In the New Testament, that Savior appeared to God's people. How do we know the Holy Bible is God's Word? *"Every Scripture is God-breathed and profitable for teaching, for reproof, for correction, and for instruction in righteousness"* (2 Tim. 3:16). In addition, prophecy was fulfilled. Only an omnipotent God could orchestrate the recording of multiple manuscripts over multiple centuries, all coming together as a cohesive narrative that not only details God's plan for us but also shows exactly how that plan has come to reality. More specifically, multiple transcribers under God's inspiration foretold Christ's coming and the details of his birth, life, death, and resurrection hundreds of years preceding the events. Here are just a few of the prophecies about Jesus's death fulfilled in scripture.

Old Testament Prophecy: *"'Awake, sword, against my shepherd, and against the man who is close to me,' says Yahweh of Armies. 'Strike the shepherd, and the sheep will be scattered; and I will turn my hand against the little ones'"* (Zech. 13:7).

New Testament Fulfillment: *"Then Jesus said to them, 'All of you will be made to stumble because of me tonight, for it is written, "I will strike the shepherd, and the sheep of the flock will be scattered"'"* (Matt. 26:31).

Old Testament Prophecy: *"Yes, my own familiar friend, in whom I trusted, who ate bread with me, has lifted up his heel against me"* (Ps. 41:9).

New Testament Fulfillment: *"While he was still speaking, a crowd appeared. He who was called Judas, one of the twelve, was leading them. He came near to Jesus to kiss him. But Jesus said to him, 'Judas, do you betray the Son of Man with a kiss?'"* (Luke 22:47–48).

Old Testament Prophecy: *"I said to them, 'If you think it best, give me my wages; and if not, keep them.' So they weighed for my wages thirty pieces of silver. Yahweh said to me, 'Throw it to the potter, the handsome price that I was valued at by them!' I took the thirty pieces of silver, and threw them to the potter, in Yahweh's house"* (Zech. 11:12–13).

New Testament Fulfillment: *"And [Judas Iscariot] said, 'What are you willing to give me if I deliver him to you?' So they weighed out for him thirty pieces of silver"* (Matt. 26:15).

"He threw down the pieces of silver in the sanctuary and departed. Then he went away and hanged himself.

The chief priests took the pieces of silver and said, 'It's not lawful to put them into the treasury, since it is the price of blood.' They took counsel, and bought the potter's field with them to bury strangers in. Therefore that field has been called "The Field of Blood" to this day. Then that which was spoken through Jeremiah the prophet was fulfilled, saying,

> *'They took the thirty pieces of silver,*
> > *the price of him upon whom a price had been set,*
> > *whom some of the children of Israel priced,*
> > *and they gave them for the potter's field,*
> > *as the Lord commanded me.'"*

> —Matt. 27:5–10

Old Testament Prophecy: *"He was oppressed, yet when he was afflicted he didn't open his mouth. As a lamb that is led to the slaughter, and as a sheep that before its shearers is silent, so he didn't open his mouth"* (Isa. 53:7).

New Testament Fulfillment: *"But he stayed quiet, and answered nothing. Again the high priest asked him, 'Are you the Christ, the Son of the Blessed?'"* (Mark 14:61).

Old Testament Prophecy: *"I gave my back to those who beat me, and my cheeks to those who plucked off the hair. I didn't hide my face from shame and spitting"* (Isa. 50:6).

New Testament Fulfillment: *"Then they spat in his face and beat him with their fists, and some slapped him"* (Matt. 26:67).

"Then he released Barabbas to them, but Jesus he flogged and delivered to be crucified" (Matt. 27:26).

Old Testament Prophecy: *"They divide my garments among them. They cast lots for my clothing"* (Ps. 22:18).

New Testament Fulfillment: *"Jesus said, 'Father, forgive them, for they don't know what they are doing.' Dividing his garments among them, they cast lots"* (Luke 23:34).

Old Testament Prophecy: *"All those who see me mock me. They insult me with their lips. They shake their heads, saying, 'He trusts in Yahweh. Let him deliver him. Let him rescue him, since he delights in him'"* (Ps. 22:7–8).

New Testament Fulfillment: *"The people stood watching. The rulers with them also scoffed at him, saying, 'He saved others. Let him save himself, if this is the Christ of God, his chosen one!'"* (Luke 23:35).

Old Testament Prophecy: *"They also gave me poison for my food. In my thirst, they gave me vinegar to drink"* (Ps. 69:21).

New Testament Fulfillment: *"After this, Jesus, seeing that all things were now finished, that the Scripture might be fulfilled, said, 'I am thirsty.' Now a vessel full of vinegar was set there; so they put a sponge full of the vinegar on hyssop, and held it at his mouth"* (John 19:28–29).

Old Testament Prophecy: *"He protects all of his bones. Not one of them is broken"* (Ps. 34:20).

New Testament Fulfillment: *"But when they came to Jesus, and saw that he was already dead, they didn't break his legs. However one of the soldiers pierced his side with a spear, and immediately blood and water came out. He who has seen has testified, and his testimony is true. He knows that he tells the truth, that you may believe. For these things happened that the Scripture might be fulfilled, 'A bone of him will not be broken'"* (John 19:33–36).

Old Testament Prophecy: *"They made his grave with the wicked, and with a rich man in his death, although he had done no violence, nor was any deceit in his mouth"* (Isa. 53:9).

New Testament Fulfillment: *"When evening had come, a rich man from Arimathaea named Joseph, who himself was also Jesus' disciple, came. This man went to Pilate and asked for Jesus' body.*

Then Pilate commanded the body to be given up. Joseph took the body and wrapped it in a clean linen cloth and laid it in his own new tomb, which he had cut out in the rock. Then he rolled a large stone against the door of the tomb, and departed" (Matt. 27:57–60).

Old Testament Prophecy: *"You have ascended on high. You have led away captives. You have received gifts among people, yes, among the rebellious also, that Yah God might dwell there"* (Ps. 68:18).

New Testament Fulfillment: *"So then the Lord, after he had spoken to them, was received up into heaven, and sat down at the right hand of God"* (Mark 16:19).

There are many other prophecies fulfilled in scripture. Most scholars count more than 300. But just to add some mathematical basis to the certainty of scripture in general and of Jesus as the Christ in particular, a book called *Science Speaks* by Peter Stoner and Robert Newman explains the probability that any one person could, purposefully or accidently, fulfill just eight (not all of them, only eight) of the biblical prophecies about Jesus as 1:100,000,000,000,000,000 (10 to the 17th power). That's as likely as finding a marked silver dollar in a pile big enough to cover a space the size of Texas.[5]

Arguably, the most important prophecy Jesus fulfilled was that of the will of the Father—that through him, all could have eternal life.

Old Testament Prophecy: *"Yet it pleased Yahweh to bruise him. He has caused him to suffer. When you make his soul an offering for sin, he will see his offspring. He will prolong his days and Yahweh's pleasure will prosper in his hand"* (Isa. 53:10).

New Testament Fulfillment: *"This is eternal life, that they should know you, the only true God, and him whom you sent, Jesus Christ"* (John 17:3).

---

5. Peter W. Stoner and Robert C. Newman, *Science Speaks: Scientific Proof of the Accuracy of Prophecy and the Bible*, revised by Don W. Stoner (Chicago: Moody Press, 2005), http://sciencespeaks.dstoner.net/Christ_of_Prophecy.html#c9.

---❖---

ONE EXPERIENCE
AND ALL IS NEW

Now concerning spiritual things, brothers, I don't want you to be ignorant. You know that when you were heathen you were led away to those mute idols, however you might be led. Therefore I make known to you that no man speaking by God's Spirit says, "Jesus is accursed." No one can say, "Jesus is Lord," but by the Holy Spirit.

Now there are various kinds of gifts, but the same Spirit. There are various kinds of service, and the same Lord. There are various kinds of workings, but the same God, who works all things in all. But to each one is given the manifestation of the Spirit for the profit of all. For to one is given through the Spirit the word of wisdom, and to another the word of knowledge, according to the same Spirit; to another faith, by the same Spirit; and to another gifts of healings, by the same Spirit; and to another workings of miracles; and to another prophecy; and to another discerning of spirits; to another different kinds of languages; and to another the interpretation of languages. But the one and the same Spirit produces all of these, distributing to each one separately as he desires.

—1 Cor. 12:1–11

But you, beloved, keep building up yourselves on your most holy faith, praying in the Holy Spirit. Keep yourselves in God's love, looking for the mercy of our Lord Jesus Christ to eternal life.

—Jude 20–21

In this chapter, I'm going to get personal and hope I don't lose anyone in the process. Recently, our daily campus newsletter started announcing an opportunity to participate in Spiritual Direction. For several days, a voice in my heart said, "You should do it." Every day, I read the e-mail and deleted it. Finally, I responded to the invitation and met with our campus minister for an hour so she could introduce the concept. During our time together, I realized my need to yield my spirit to God and let him drive. (By the way, remember those bumper stickers that said, "God is my co-pilot"? I've learned that if God is the co-pilot, I'm in the wrong seat!) Our minister suggested a time she called a "holy pause." The intent is to listen for God's direction. For as long as I can remember, I've felt I could hear God's voice, but this was an opportunity to do more.

I feel I have a strong, intellectual relationship with God. In other words, I'm fairly book-smart. But I also know that I need to grow in my active relationship with God. Throughout my life, I've studied Bible stories, study tips, and commentaries to understand scripture. But there are scriptures that I wasn't taught much about—specifically verses about the gifts of the Spirit. I was never told the gifts of the Spirit were a priority. When we moved from Arkansas City, Kansas, we didn't find a Christian Church (Disciples of Christ) in Poteau, Oklahoma. We attended a non-denominational church, and there, for the first time, I heard someone pray in a prayer language. It was not scary or uncomfortable, but it was something I had never heard before. When we lived in Edmond, Oklahoma, I worked for an International Pentecostal Holiness Church university and attended a meeting in Oklahoma City held by Andrew Wommack. In that meeting, he prayed in a prayer language for a brief part of the service. He regularly encouraged the gifts of the Spirit in his teachings. As part of that meeting, he gave away a book called *The New You & the Holy Spirit*. I promptly took the book home and laid it on the table beside my chair. And there it lay.

As I've studied over the last several years, it became apparent to me that my intellectual faith was missing something. I'd considered the value of praying in a prayer language, but I'd done nothing to learn how, assuming God would just drop it on me if he wanted me to do so. My meeting with our campus minister changed that.

As we practiced the holy pause, it became painfully apparent to me that even in a time of silence (pause), I was trying to control the situation. I was supposed to be listening, but I was doing the talking in my head. I realized then that I had not yielded my spirit to God—maybe somewhat, but not completely. I considered that notion as a possible reason for other situations in my life. I could talk a good talk, but I had not given God complete control of my spirit, a spirit that is supposed to be the same as Christ's. *"But he who is spiritual discerns all things, and he himself is judged by no one. 'For who has known the mind of the Lord, that he should instruct him?' But we have Christ's mind"* (1 Cor. 2:15–16). I left her office determined to yield my spirit. (Is it an oxymoron to determine to yield?)

My normal routine is to get up in the morning and go straight to my computer. I have a great Holy Bible study software that lets me read scripture and its related commentary by several different authors. I also have found a few commentaries on the Internet that I feel are well-researched and helpful. That week, I decided not to spend time in my normal study but rather read *The New You & the Holy Spirit*. It was the right time to read the book. I was ready to hear the message. I finished it in a few days—just in time, as it turned out.

That day as I headed out for work, I decided to put the practices of the book into action. In the book, Wommack shares the value of receiving the Holy Spirit. I had heard of this idea from him several times and also from other speakers I listen to on a regular basis, so I agreed with what I was reading. He finally got to the part I needed to hear—the *how*. He outlined his first experience, and I modeled my morning drive after it. He included a couple of prayers I didn't repeat word for word but followed in substance. In those prayers, I thanked God for giving the Holy Spirit as our helper. I thanked God for allowing the Holy Spirit to actually move in and direct my spirit if I would let him. I thanked him for giving me the ability to pray in a prayer language.

This is where I had become stuck in my previous half-hearted attempts: I hadn't done anything. I figured it would just happen. But now I knew I had to do something. I had to make sounds. I had no idea what sounds to make, but the book said to speak until it felt right. There came out of my mouth (not just in my head) sounds that sounded or felt right. I repeated those sounds over and over and added new ones. Eventually I had another sound that felt right, and then another. By the time I turned onto the highway between Arkansas City and Winfield, Kansas, I had three sounds. I repeated them over and over in no particular order, sometimes one sound multiple times, sometimes all in a row, with no pattern.

While I was repeating these sounds, I checked my rearview mirror and saw a silver Ford Focus coming up fast behind me. The highway was four lanes, but we were both in the same lane. I continued to repeat the sounds and watch in the mirror. In just a few seconds, the car was on me and not slowing down. I realized I had to make a move and started to change lanes, half expecting to be slammed in the tailgate while doing so. Just as I was ready to move, the car darted hard into the grass. I had my speed control set on the speed limit, 70 miles per hour. He was going so fast that he passed me in the grass! I watched in the mirror as he pulled to a stop and sat for a few seconds. As I looked for a place to turn around and go check on him, he pulled back onto the highway. He got back up to speed and then exited at the next corner. I could only assume that he was headed home and had fallen asleep. What I also assumed was that he was likely going fast enough for his car to go under my truck, likely lifting the rear wheels off the ground. From that point, anything could have happened, and it would not have been good for either of us.

But I know for a fact what *did* happen. As I was repeating those sounds, letting my spirit communicate with God, God sent this fellow safely around my truck, and no one was hurt. At that particular spot in the road, there were no road signs, ruts, or holes—only smooth shoulder. It was God's supernatural provision for both of us.

God's timing is perfect. That day was the day I finally took action and learned to commune with God in a realm I did not understand.

> *For he who speaks in another language speaks not to men, but to God; for no one understands; but in the Spirit he speaks mysteries.*
>
> —1 Cor. 14:2

> *For if I pray in another language, my spirit prays, but my understanding is unfruitful.*
>
> —1 Cor. 14:14

Whether I was praying for protection for myself, the stranger driving behind me, or something else entirely, I do not know. But I know that God performs miracles today because I saw it and experienced it.

Some people who are more experienced in prayer language might interpret that experience differently, but no one can convince me that yielding my spirit to God's and that car moving around me were not related.

———❖———

NO

DOUBT

*When he entered again into Capernaum after some days,
it was heard that he was at home. Immediately many were
gathered together, so that there was no more room, not even
around the door; and he spoke the word to them. Four people
came, carrying a paralytic to him. When they could not come
near to him for the crowd, they removed the roof where he
was. When they had broken it up, they let down the mat that
the paralytic was lying on. Jesus, seeing their faith, said to the
paralytic, "Son, your sins are forgiven you."*

*But there were some of the scribes sitting there and
reasoning in their hearts, "Why does this man speak
blasphemies like that? Who can forgive sins but God alone?"*

*Immediately Jesus, perceiving in his spirit that they so
reasoned within themselves, said to them, "Why do you reason
these things in your hearts? Which is easier, to tell the paralytic,
'Your sins are forgiven;' or to say, 'Arise, and take up your bed,
and walk?' But that you may know that the Son of Man has
authority on earth to forgive sins"—he said to the paralytic—"I
tell you, arise, take up your mat, and go to your house."*

*He arose, and immediately took up the mat and went out
in front of them all, so that they were all amazed and glorified
God, saying, "We never saw anything like this!"*

—Mark 2:1–12

He went with him [Jairus], and a great multitude followed him, and they pressed upon him on all sides. A certain woman, who had a discharge of blood for twelve years, and had suffered many things by many physicians, and had spent all that she had, and was no better, but rather grew worse, having heard the things concerning Jesus, came up behind him in the crowd, and touched his clothes. For she said, "If I just touch his clothes, I will be made well." Immediately the flow of her blood was dried up, and she felt in her body that she was healed of her affliction.

Immediately Jesus, perceiving in himself that the power had gone out from him, turned around in the crowd, and asked, "Who touched my clothes?"

His disciples said to him, "You see the multitude pressing against you, and you say, 'Who touched me?'"

He looked around to see her who had done this thing. But the woman, fearing and trembling, knowing what had been done to her, came and fell down before him, and told him all the truth.

He said to her, "Daughter, your faith has made you well. Go in peace, and be cured of your disease."

—Mark 5:24–34

Mark is the Gospel I typically go back to the least; I can't explain why. But when I do, all kinds of things jump out at me. For instance, in the two passages above are two phenomenal stories of faith, belief, and humility.

In the first passage, a paralyzed man came to Jesus, who had already established a reputation for powerful teaching and healing those in need. This man was but one in a crowd. He had faith that Jesus could heal him, but how could he reach Jesus? Four of his friends tried to carry him to Jesus, but the crowd was just too much. So they did what anyone would do (yeah, right). They took their friend up on the roof, made a hole, and lowered him right down in front of Jesus.

Many might see this as arrogant or aggressive, but they were humbling themselves and the paralyzed man by not caring what others thought or said about them. They cared about what Jesus said. They had faith that Jesus *could* heal and that he *would* heal. Faith was their focus. They put their faith into action for their friend, not for themselves. The paralyzed man also humbled himself when Jesus told him to pick up the mat and walk. He didn't care what others would say or think if he stumbled, fell, or couldn't get up. He cared what Jesus said. He had faith, and he put his faith into action.

In the second passage, the woman with a hemorrhage came to Jesus and found a similar situation. The crowds around him kept her at a distance. She had tried everything to be healed and had spent all she had on doctors. But she had faith in Jesus's ability to heal her—so much faith, in fact, that she believed all she had to do was touch the very hem of his clothes and she would be healed. As a person with a hemorrhage, she would have been unclean according to Jewish law. For this reason, she took a big chance to work her way through the crowd, which probably explains her reluctance to admit she was the one who had touched him. She received healing from Jesus because of her faith, but she ultimately received his full blessing by humbling herself, by not worrying what others might think or say about her, and by trusting him.

Let's look at some interpretations of specific words. First, let's look at the word *faith*. Many say it means an unwavering belief in something or someone. Scripture says this about faith: *"Now faith is assurance of things hoped for, proof of things not seen"* (Heb. 11:1). And the source of faith is this: *"So faith comes by hearing, and hearing by the word of God"* (Rom. 10:17). Belief is confidence in some concept, person, or thing. So is there a discernible difference between faith and belief? For me, it's a head versus heart kind of thing. Maybe the best way to describe the difference is to use unbelief as an example. I think most will say they have faith that God *can* (heart), but most also do not believe that God *will* (head). And why would they? When we compare our relative worthiness to others' or God's standards, we see ourselves as unworthy. Such thinking is pride.

How can it be pride? Pride is putting yourself ahead of God. "But I'm not doing that," you might argue. "Saying I'm not worthy is not putting myself first." I think it is. Pride is looking to the world first, thinking about how we think or feel, and not trusting the Word for what it says. The Word says we are worthy not because of us but because of what Jesus has done for us. *"For him who knew no sin he made to be sin on our behalf; so that in him we might become the righteousness of God"* (2 Cor. 5:21).

We are clearly physical beings. We see, hear, feel, smell, and taste in the physical world. The world we live in has made most of us skeptical and cynical. We have learned that it isn't always smart or safe to trust what we hear, see, or read. But we are also spiritual beings, and we must learn to be *primarily* spiritual beings. When we trust what we can see, hear, feel, taste, and smell more than we trust the Word of God, we are being physical (carnal). When we worry about what others will think of us if we speak up, believe what the Holy Bible says, or dare to go a different direction from the crowd, we are being physical. When we doubt that God has only the best intentions for us, we are being physical. And all these practices are rooted in pride.

God's Word says to put him first and listen to his voice only. Whom do you trust—the world or God? Whom do you allow to influence your thoughts—the world or God?

We must allow ourselves to trust God's Word and let God influence our thoughts and actions, *"for we walk by faith, not by sight"* (2 Cor. 5:7). This is the fine line between faith and belief. Doubts of any kind are not of God. *"Jesus answered them, 'Most certainly I tell you, if you have faith and don't doubt, you will not only do what was done to the fig tree, but even if you told this mountain, "Be taken up and cast into the sea," it would be done. All things, whatever you ask in prayer, believing, you will receive'"* (Matt. 21:21–22). Doubts are the devil's thoughts. Remember, the enemy comes to destroy (John 10:10), and doubt will destroy faith.

There is a practical lesson from these two passages. Humble yourselves so you trust not your own thoughts but God's Word. *"Trust in Yahweh with all your heart, and don't lean on your own understanding.*

In all your ways acknowledge him, and he will make your paths straight" (Prov. 3:5–6). The paralyzed man and his friends and the woman with the hemorrhage all had faith that Jesus not only *could* heal them but that he *would* heal them. If you have doubts of any kind about the validity of the promises in God's Word or wonder whether you are worthy, put those thoughts away. *"He himself bore our sins in his body on the tree, that we, having died to sins, might live to righteousness. You were healed by his wounds"* (1 Pet. 2:24). Notice the tense of the verb *were healed*. Healing has already happened! And *healed* is an all-encompassing word—physically, emotionally, spiritually, relationally, and financially. It is done. Don't let doubt, which is of the devil, steal that away.

> *But if any of you lacks wisdom, let him ask of God, who gives to all liberally and without reproach, and it will be given to him. But let him ask in faith, without any doubting, for he who doubts is like a wave of the sea, driven by the wind and tossed. For that man shouldn't think that he will receive anything from the Lord. He is a double-minded man, unstable in all his ways.*
>
> —James 1:5–8

AS GOD IN CHRIST
HAS FORGIVEN YOU

Then Peter came and said to him, "Lord, how often shall my brother sin against me, and I forgive him? Until seven times?"

Jesus said to him, "I don't tell you until seven times, but, until seventy times seven. Therefore the Kingdom of Heaven is like a certain king, who wanted to settle accounts with his servants. When he had begun to settle, one was brought to him who owed him ten thousand talents. But because he couldn't pay, his lord commanded him to be sold, with his wife, his children, and all that he had, and payment to be made. The servant therefore fell down and knelt before him, saying, 'Lord, have patience with me, and I will repay you all!' The lord of that servant, being moved with compassion, released him and forgave him the debt.

"But that servant went out and found one of his fellow servants who owed him one hundred denarii, and he grabbed him and took him by the throat, saying, 'Pay me what you owe!'

"So his fellow servant fell down at his feet and begged him, saying, 'Have patience with me, and I will repay you!' He would not, but went and cast him into prison until he should pay back that which was due. So when his fellow servants saw what was done, they were exceedingly sorry, and came and

told their lord all that was done. Then his lord called him in and said to him, 'You wicked servant! I forgave you all that debt because you begged me. Shouldn't you also have had mercy on your fellow servant, even as I had mercy on you?' His lord was angry, and delivered him to the tormentors until he should pay all that was due to him. So my heavenly Father will also do to you, if you don't each forgive your brother from your hearts for his misdeeds."

—Matt. 18:21–35

I was amazed when someone once told me, "I will never be able to forgive them." I thought, "But you're a Christian!" Then I thought, "I guess you won't, not if you don't want to." Finally, I concluded that maybe I shouldn't speak so quickly.

Several years ago, I was denied a job I thought I would be good at. In fact, I had been filling in at the position for several months. When I didn't get the job, I was hurt—so hurt that I left the state and started my work life over. I told myself I was "clearing the path" for new blood (and I still believe there is an element of truth in that), but when I look back now, it was mostly my pride speaking. Every time I had to go back to Arkansas City, Kansas, my stomach tightened. I did not want to be there. That sentiment hung around for several years and was still there when we moved back to Arkansas City not long ago.

I think it is a natural reaction of our soul (mind, will, and emotions) to try to protect us when we get hurt, be it mentally, professionally, or physically. We may get angry, depressed, lonely, or combative. Or we might just give up. But God has a different plan.

Before the events in the verses above, Jesus was teaching the disciples how to reconcile with a fellow believer. He told them to confront the offending brother directly. If that failed, then they should take two or three witnesses with them. If that also failed, they should take the issue to the whole church. The idea was to save the relationship. In the above passage, Peter asks how many times we should forgive, boldly and confidently offering seven as the answer to his own question. But Jesus said, *"I don't tell you until seven times, but, until seventy times seven."* Some translations reverse the words and say 77 times, but either number is meant to say to us, "Forgive until you mean it." Jesus then showed them via the parable an example of extravagant forgiveness.

For perspective, a talent was a weight measurement and equal to about 75 pounds. You can do the math and see that if the servant owed 75 pounds of silver (or, even greater, 75 pounds of gold), he had a lifetime's worth of debt—probably several lifetimes. To pay the debt, the servant was ordered to make his lifetime's worth of payment as a slave. In fact, he would make several lifetime payments, for his wife and children would become slaves as well. But the master was moved to compassion when the servant fell down and begged for mercy. Not only did the master free him from slavery, but he also completely forgave the debt—all of it.

Shortly after, the servant found a fellow who owed him 100 denarii (or 100 pence in other translations), about 100 days' wages or a few months of debt. The fellow fell down and begged for mercy. The servant had the opportunity to show the same mercy and compassion that his master had shown him, but he did not. Instead, he ignored the fellow's plea and had him thrown into prison.

When the master heard what the forgiven servant did, he was outraged. He instantly turned the servant over to the tormentors. The last verse ends with a stern warning: *"So my heavenly Father will also do to you, if you don't each forgive your brother from your hearts for his misdeeds."* This verse isn't a lone example. Here are some similar verses.

For if you forgive men their trespasses, your heavenly Father will also forgive you. But if you don't forgive men their trespasses, neither will your Father forgive your trespasses.
—Matt. 6:14–15

Whenever you stand praying, forgive, if you have anything against anyone; so that your Father, who is in heaven, may also forgive you your transgressions.
—Mark 11:25

> *Don't judge,*
>   *and you won't be judged.*
> *Don't condemn,*
>   *and you won't be condemned.*
> *Set free,*
>   *and you will be set free.*

> *Give, and it will be given to you: good measure, pressed down, shaken together, and running over, will be given to you. For with the same measure you measure it will be measured back to you.*
> —Luke 6:37–38

God expects us to forgive others. Paul continues the thought.

> *Bearing with one another, and forgiving each other, if any man has a complaint against any; even as Christ forgave you, so you also do.*
> —Col. 3:13

> *Let all bitterness, wrath, anger, outcry, and slander be put away from you, with all malice. And be kind to one another, tender hearted, forgiving each other, just as God also in Christ forgave you.*
> —Eph. 4:31–32

To be forgiven, we must forgive others. So do we earn God's forgiveness of sin when we forgive others? And what if we forgive but don't have reconciliation? Ephesians 1:7 explains, *"In whom we have our redemption through his blood, the forgiveness of our trespasses, according to the riches of his grace."* Jesus has already died for our sins, including the sin of unforgiveness. But read this passage.

> *Turning to the woman, he said to Simon, "Do you see this woman? I entered into your house, and you gave me no water*

for my feet, but she has wet my feet with her tears, and wiped
them with the hair of her head. You gave me no kiss, but she,
since the time I came in, has not ceased to kiss my feet. You
didn't anoint my head with oil, but she has anointed my feet
with ointment. Therefore I tell you, her sins, which are many,
are forgiven, for she loved much. But one to whom little is
forgiven, loves little." He said to her, "Your sins are forgiven."
—Luke 7:44–48

Sometimes, we may feel that because we are relatively good people, we have been forgiven little, and therefore we forgive little. However, scripture clearly indicates that we must forgive others because we have been forgiven. The master expected his servant to forgive his debtor as he had been forgiven. The servant was forgiven first before he had the opportunity to forgive others. Our confession of Jesus as our Lord and Savior means we are forgiven.

But when the servant did not forgive, the master turned the servant over to be tormented (some translations say tortured). Think about that for a minute. The debt was forgiven, but the servant was faced with torment. I've heard it said before that refusing to forgive someone else is like drinking poison and expecting the person we have not forgiven to die. We are tormented if we don't forgive. Why? Refusing forgiveness gives a place for the devil, and you can safely bet that he will torment us.

We must trust in the source of our forgiveness and focus on Christ only. Remember, the debt the servant owed was several lifetimes' worth of debt. He could never have repaid it, even if he had dedicated his life to it. Does that scenario sound familiar? Our sin is like several lifetimes' worth of debt we could never repay. Ah, but it has been paid, completely forgiven, at the cost of Jesus's life.

I carried bitterness (a form of unforgiveness) around for several years, but not anymore. Now I live and work around the ones who snubbed me (in reality, probably the best thing that ever happened to me). I grew tired of the torment. Studying and applying the Word have forced me to take scripture for what it says, not what I would like it to say. I trust that God is with me, and I savor that trust. It's hard to savor anything when you are tormented. If you are withholding forgiveness from anyone, forgive them, and let it go. Remember the woman in the Luke passage. She loved much because she had been forgiven much. As a follower and believer of Christ, you and I have been forgiven much, a lifetime's worth of debt, and our response to that forgiveness should be much love as well.

---❖---

THE POWER
OF GOD'S WORD

For nothing spoken by God is impossible.

—Luke 1:37

To be consistent with the rest of the book, the verse above is from the World English Bible. But one study I have uses the American Standard Version, the version that inspired this writing.

For no word from God shall be void of power.

—Luke 1:37 (ASV)

In this verse, the angel Gabriel was responding to the Virgin Mary's question, *"How shall this be?"* (Luke 1:34, ASV). God's words are imminently truthful and powerful. I've selected a few words God spoke in the Old Testament.

> *In the beginning, God created the heavens and the earth. The earth was formless and empty. Darkness was on the surface of the deep and God's Spirit was hovering over the surface of the waters.*
>
> *God said, "Let there be light," and there was light. God saw the light, and saw that it was good. God divided the light from the darkness. God called the light "day", and the darkness he called "night". There was evening and there was morning, the first day.*

God said, "Let there be an expanse in the middle of the waters, and let it divide the waters from the waters." God made the expanse, and divided the waters which were under the expanse from the waters which were above the expanse; and it was so. God called the expanse "sky". There was evening and there was morning, a second day.

God said, "Let the waters under the sky be gathered together to one place, and let the dry land appear;" and it was so. God called the dry land "earth", and the gathering together of the waters he called "seas". God saw that it was good. God said, "Let the earth yield grass, herbs yielding seeds, and fruit trees bearing fruit after their kind, with their seeds in it, on the earth;" and it was so. The earth yielded grass, herbs yielding seed after their kind, and trees bearing fruit, with their seeds in it, after their kind; and God saw that it was good. There was evening and there was morning, a third day.

God said, "Let there be lights in the expanse of the sky to divide the day from the night; and let them be for signs to mark seasons, days, and years; and let them be for lights in the expanse of the sky to give light on the earth;" and it was so. God made the two great lights: the greater light to rule the day, and the lesser light to rule the night. He also made the stars. God set them in the expanse of the sky to give light to the earth, and to rule over the day and over the night, and to divide the light from the darkness. God saw that it was good. There was evening and there was morning, a fourth day.

God said, "Let the waters abound with living creatures, and let birds fly above the earth in the open expanse of the sky." God created the large sea creatures and every living creature that moves, with which the waters swarmed, after their kind, and every winged bird after its kind. God saw that it was good. God blessed them, saying, "Be fruitful, and multiply, and fill the waters in the seas, and let birds *multiply on the earth." There was evening and there was morning, a fifth day.*

God said, "Let the earth produce living creatures after their kind, livestock, creeping things, and animals of the earth after their kind;" and it was so. God made the animals of the earth after their kind, and the livestock after their kind, and everything that creeps on the ground after its kind. God saw that it was good.

God said, "Let's make man in our image, after our likeness. Let them have dominion over the fish of the sea, and over the birds of the sky, and over the livestock, and over all the earth, and over every creeping thing that creeps on the earth." God created man in his own image. In God's image he created him; male and female he created them. God blessed them. God said to them, "Be fruitful, multiply, fill the earth, and subdue it. Have dominion over the fish of the sea, over the birds of the sky, and over every living thing that moves on the earth." God said, "Behold, I have given you every herb yielding seed, which is on the surface of all the earth, and every tree, which bears fruit yielding seed. It will be your food. To every animal of the earth, and to every bird of the sky, and to everything that creeps on the earth, in which there is life, I have given every green herb for food;" and it was so.

God saw everything that he had made, and, behold, it was very good. There was evening and there was morning, a sixth day.
—Gen. 1:1–31

Don't you be afraid, for I am with you.
 Don't be dismayed, for I am your God.
 I will strengthen you.
 Yes, I will help you.
 Yes, I will uphold you with the right hand of my
 righteousness.
—Isa. 41:10

For I, Yahweh your God, will hold your right hand,
  saying to you, "Don't be afraid.
  I will help you."

—Isa. 41:13

"For the mountains may depart,
  and the hills be removed;
but my loving kindness will not depart from you,
  and my covenant of peace will not be removed,"
says Yahweh who has mercy on you.

—Isa. 54:10

"Bring the whole tithe into the storehouse, that there may be food in my house, and test me now in this," says Yahweh of Armies, "if I will not open you the windows of heaven, and pour you out a blessing, that there will not be room enough for."

—Mal. 3:10

Can you name any more powerful words than those spoken when God created all? Just imagine the force of words that can make everything from nothing! It was dark, and God spoke light into existence. There were no planets, sky, land, water, or animals. God created everything with powerful words. And he not only created, but he said his creation was good. Then he created mankind in his own image. He gave man dominion over all things and called it very good. Think about that for a minute. We often take creation for granted because it has always been. But try to build this picture in your mind—there was nothing. Perhaps the closest you can imagine is total darkness.

I went to Alabaster Caverns in northwestern Oklahoma when I was a kid. Included in the tour of the main cave were a few seconds of total darkness. Nothing was visible. Imagine nothing visible—no place, space, or time. Then imagine God's voice commanding creation into existence. He didn't mix any ingredients or wave his hands. He simply spoke. *"For no word from God shall be void of power"* (Luke 1:37 ASV). How less powerful

154

are his words when he says that he holds our hand, that his love will never depart from us, and that we should not fear? They are no less than his promise to pour down overflowing blessing if we will only bring the full tithe into the storehouse. Note that the verse from Malachi above is the only verse in all of scripture where God says, *"Put me to the test."*

Let's expand this topic. Of course, all scripture is God's Word, and we know from John 1 that Jesus is the Word personified.

> *In the beginning was the Word, and the Word was with God, and the Word was God. The same was in the beginning with God. All things were made through him. Without him, nothing was made that has been made. In him was life, and the life was the light of men. The light shines in the darkness, and the darkness hasn't overcome it.*
>
> —John 1:1–5

Jesus's word is the same as God's word. It has the same power. Keep in mind God's powerful word in creation, and consider these selections of Jesus's words.

> *"I am the Alpha and the Omega," says the Lord God, "who is and who was and who is to come, the Almighty."*
>
> —Rev. 1:8

> *Again, therefore, Jesus spoke to them, saying, "I am the light of the world. He who follows me will not walk in the darkness, but will have the light of life."*
>
> —John 8:12

> *Jesus said to her, "I am the resurrection and the life. He who believes in me will still live, even if he dies. Whoever lives and believes in me will never die. Do you believe this?"*
>
> —John 11:25–26

Jesus said to him, "I am the way, the truth, and the life. No one comes to the Father, except through me."

—John 14:6

Therefore don't be anxious, saying, "What will we eat?", "What will we drink?" or, "With what will we be clothed?" For the Gentiles seek after all these things; for your heavenly Father knows that you need all these things. But seek first God's Kingdom and his righteousness; and all these things will be given to you as well.

—Matt. 6:31–33

Come to me, all you who labor and are heavily burdened, and I will give you rest. Take my yoke upon you and learn from me, for I am gentle and humble in heart; and you will find rest for your souls.

—Matt. 11:28–29

I tell you, keep asking, and it will be given you. Keep seeking, and you will find. Keep knocking, and it will be opened to you. For everyone who asks receives. He who seeks finds. To him who knocks it will be opened.

—Luke 11:9–10

Don't let your heart be troubled. Believe in God. Believe also in me. In my Father's house are many homes. If it weren't so, I would have told you. I am going to prepare a place for you. If I go and prepare a place for you, I will come again, and will receive you to myself; that where I am, you may be there also.

—John 14:1–3

Behold, I send out the promise of my Father on you. But wait in the city of Jerusalem until you are clothed with power from on high.

—Luke 24:49

"Go and make disciples of all nations, baptizing them in the name of the Father and of the Son and of the Holy Spirit, teaching them to observe all things that I commanded you. Behold, I am with you always, even to the end of the age." Amen.

—Matt. 28:19–20

As God lovingly spoke creation, promises, and blessing, so Jesus echoes that love. He reassures us that because he is the light of the world, we will no longer have darkness. He promises us everlasting life through him. He promises his provision, presence, and rest. His Word tells us that he has prepared a place for us, a place with him and the Father. He promises a helper for today, the Holy Spirit. And to receive all these promises, we have but to seek them through him. *"For no word from God shall be void of power."*

When you're experiencing unfamiliar, uncomfortable, worrisome, or even scary times when it feels as though you're standing against everyone around you, remember that God is holding your hand. He promised he would never leave you. All his words are true and powerful. *"For no word from God shall be void of power."* Take comfort in the fact that he has already won. The victory is yours through Jesus.

I have told you these things, that in me you may have peace. In the world you have trouble; but cheer up! I have overcome the world.

—John 16:33

When I saw him, I fell at his feet like a dead man.

He laid his right hand on me, saying, "Don't be afraid. I am the first and the last, and the Living one. I was dead, and behold, I am alive forever and ever. Amen. I have the keys of Death and of Hades."

—Rev. 1:17–18

The devil who deceived them was thrown into the lake of fire and sulfur, where the beast and the false prophet are also. They will be tormented day and night forever and ever.

—Rev. 20:10

I heard a loud voice out of heaven saying, "Behold, God's dwelling is with people, and he will dwell with them, and they will be his people, and God himself will be with them as their God. He will wipe away every tear from their eyes. Death will be no more; neither will there be mourning, nor crying, nor pain, any more. The first things have passed away."

He who sits on the throne said, "Behold, I am making all things new." He said, "Write, for these words of God are faithful and true." He said to me, "I am the Alpha and the Omega, the Beginning and the End. I will give freely to him who is thirsty from the spring of the water of life. He who overcomes, I will give him these things. I will be his God, and he will be my son."

—Rev. 21:3–7

Trust him at his word, and savor the trust. Just as you enjoy your favorite meal, delight yourself in trusting him who created all, who sent his only Son, who became one of us, took on all our sin and suffering, and died so that eternal heaven might be ours. Savor the trust you have in our Almighty God!

✦

THE
LIGHTHOUSE

Again, therefore, Jesus spoke to them, saying, "I am the light of the world. He who follows me will not walk in the darkness, but will have the light of life."

—John 8:12

The city has no need for the sun or moon to shine, for the very glory of God illuminated it, and its lamp is the Lamb.

—Rev. 21:23

The light shines in the darkness, and the darkness hasn't overcome it.

—John 1:5

When I was a kid, every Sunday morning before we went to church, we watched a program on television called *Gospel Jubilee!* As you would expect from my background (even though I think Dad was actually the one who turned it on), it was a Southern Gospel music show. One of the songs they sang with some regularity was "The Lighthouse," written in 1970 by Ronny Hinson. Just recently, a group made up of Jimmy Fortune, Ben Isaacs, Bradley Walker, and Mike Rogers performed the song on *Larry's Country Diner* on RFD-TV. I hadn't heard it for years, but the chorus had stuck in my mind all that time. This time, what jumped out to me was the second verse.

The lighthouse represents God's Word through Jesus. The song begins by extolling the virtues of the lighthouse, proclaiming it a way-finder in the dark and a protector from the rocky shores of life as we try to navigate tumultuous currents. Clearly, without the light from the lighthouse, our ship would have crashed long ago.

Several verses from the Holy Bible state that Jesus is the light of the world. But what does that mean to us? His light is to be our path, our way, our direction. The psalmists, speaking to God, said, *"Oh, send out your light and your truth. Let them lead me. Let them bring me to your holy hill, to your tents"* (Ps. 43:3) and *"Your word is a lamp to my feet, and a light for my path"* (Ps. 119:105). As sailors look to the lighthouse, we must look to Christ and safely follow the light home to him.

The second verse discusses a culture that says, "Tear it down! We don't need it anymore." I can't think of a modern time when society shouted any stronger, "Tear him down! We don't need him anymore!" That not only deeply saddens me but also scares me for future generations. The church in its broad sense has a large burden to bear. We have tried to make the gospel story into something it is not, and in the process, we've taken growth, responsibility, and consequence out of the narrative.

Hear the burden God put on Jeremiah to prophesy to the people of Israel. He was a lone voice in a sea of opposing ideas.

> *Yahweh says to this people,*
> *"Even so they have loved to wander.*
> *They have not restrained their feet.*
> *Therefore Yahweh does not accept them.*
> *Now he will remember their iniquity,*
> *and punish them for their sins."*

> *Yahweh said to me, "Don't pray for this people for their good. When they fast, I will not hear their cry; and when they offer burnt offering and meal offering, I will not accept them; but I will consume them by the sword, by famine, and by pestilence."*

Then I said, "Ah, Lord Yahweh! Behold, the prophets tell them, 'You will not see the sword, neither will you have famine; but I will give you assured peace in this place.'"

Then Yahweh said to me, "The prophets prophesy lies in my name. I didn't send them. I didn't command them. I didn't speak to them. They prophesy to you a lying vision, divination, and a thing of nothing, and the deceit of their own heart."

—Jer. 14:10–14

Much like many in the church (the body of believers) today, the prophets were telling the people what they wanted to hear—that because they wore the label Nation of Israel, they would not suffer consequences for ignoring God's law. But God told Jeremiah that the other prophets were deceiving the people and that Jeremiah must stay with the message—repent, for judgment is at hand. But the church today has concentrated so strongly on God's grace to us that we have forgotten the required response to grace.

Certainly, we are saved by grace, as Paul states so clearly. *"For by grace you have been saved through faith, and that not of yourselves; it is the gift of God, not of works, that no one would boast"* (Eph. 2:8–9). But James just as clearly states that grace is not all there is; works still have a part. *"What good is it, my brothers, if a man says he has faith, but has no works? Can faith save him? And if a brother or sister is naked and in lack of daily food, and one of you tells them, 'Go in peace. Be warmed and filled;' yet you didn't give them the things the body needs, what good is it? Even so faith, if it has no works, is dead in itself"* (James 2:14–17). Works, in this case, are not just what we do for our fellow brothers and sisters but also what each of us must do to be more like Christ in our thoughts and deeds.

There are ministers who continue to call people to repentance, or at least to follow God's Word in its full context. They maintain that there are standards and that some activities are sin. These ministers are generally not well received by culture because culture doesn't want to hear it. Culture wants to hear that God is love and that Jesus healed and forgave all. And those are true statements, but forgiveness is not the end of the story.

When did Jesus ever say, "You are forgiven; now go back to your sin"? On the contrary, remember the story of the woman caught in adultery?

> *The scribes and the Pharisees brought a woman taken in adultery. Having set her in the middle, they told him, "Teacher, we found this woman in adultery, in the very act. Now in our law, Moses commanded us to stone such women. What then do you say about her?" They said this testing him, that they might have something to accuse him of.*
>
> *But Jesus stooped down and wrote on the ground with his finger. But when they continued asking him, he looked up and said to them, "He who is without sin among you, let him throw the first stone at her." Again he stooped down and wrote on the ground with his finger.*
>
> *They, when they heard it, being convicted by their conscience, went out one by one, beginning from the oldest, even to the last. Jesus was left alone with the woman where she was, in the middle. Jesus, standing up, saw her and said, "Woman, where are your accusers? Did no one condemn you?"*
>
> *She said, "No one, Lord."*
>
> *Jesus said, "Neither do I condemn you. Go your way. From now on, sin no more."*
>
> —John 8:3–11

Yes, Jesus showed compassion on her and forgave her. Forgiveness is powerful for us still today. We should love and forgive because we're commanded to do so. *"He who doesn't love doesn't know God, for God is love"* (1 John 4:8). But Jesus didn't leave it at that, and the church today can't either. Culture has dismissed the influence of the church today because the church has stopped expecting change in us.

> *This is the judgment, that the light has come into the world, and men loved the darkness rather than the light; for their works were evil. For everyone who does evil hates the light,*

and doesn't come to the light, lest his works would be exposed. But he who does the truth comes to the light, that his works may be revealed, that they have been done in God.

—John 3:19–21

This is the message which we have heard from him and announce to you, that God is light, and in him is no darkness at all. If we say that we have fellowship with him and walk in the darkness, we lie, and don't tell the truth. But if we walk in the light, as he is in the light, we have fellowship with one another, and the blood of Jesus Christ, his Son, cleanses us from all sin. If we say that we have no sin, we deceive ourselves, and the truth is not in us. If we confess our sins, he is faithful and righteous to forgive us the sins, and to cleanse us from all unrighteousness.

—1 John 1:5–9

If we confess Jesus as Lord and Savior, we are made righteous for his name's sake. But we are expected to follow his light, not just acknowledge that the light exists.

So, then, my beloved brothers, let every man be swift to hear, slow to speak, and slow to anger; for the anger of man doesn't produce the righteousness of God. Therefore, putting away all filthiness and overflowing of wickedness, receive with humility the implanted word, which is able to save your souls. But be doers of the word, and not only hearers, deluding your own selves. For if anyone is a hearer of the word and not a doer, he is like a man looking at his natural face in a mirror; for he sees himself, and goes away, and immediately forgets what kind of man he was. But he who looks into the perfect law of freedom and continues, not being a hearer who forgets, but a doer of the work, this man will be blessed in what he does.

—James 1:19–25

We must strive each day to be more like Christ, and we must hold those we love to the same standard. Allowing them to continue in unrepentant sin is sin on our own hands.

> Brothers, even if a man is caught in some fault, you who are spiritual must restore such a one in a spirit of gentleness; looking to yourself so that you also aren't tempted. Bear one another's burdens, and so fulfill the law of Christ.
> —Gal. 6:1–2

> Brothers, if any among you wanders from the truth and someone turns him back, let him know that he who turns a sinner from the error of his way will save a soul from death and will cover a multitude of sins.
> —James 5:19–20

As I've said before, I used to be part of a study group that ignored verses it didn't like. These two verses from James were in that group of ignored verses. In fact, they are commonly ignored (or just unknown) by the church. We must not be passive with our brothers and sisters in Christ, and at the same time, we must not be judgmental. As noted above in 1 John 1, we know that none of us are without sin. As we are to gently correct our brothers and sisters if we really care about them, we should expect the same from them if they really care about us.

Thank God for the Lighthouse! Don't let the culture around you convince you that the Lighthouse no longer has a purpose. We need his light now, as much if not more than ever. As Jesus is the light of the world, he commanded us to be light as well.

> You are the light of the world. A city located on a hill can't be hidden. Neither do you light a lamp and put it under a measuring basket, but on a stand; and it shines to all who are in the house. Even so, let your light shine before men, that they may see your good works and glorify your Father who is in heaven.
> —Matt. 5:14–16

For so has the Lord commanded us, saying,
  "I have set you as a light for the Gentiles,
    that you should bring salvation to the uttermost parts
    of the earth."

—Acts 13:47

For you were once darkness, but are now light in the Lord. Walk as children of light, for the fruit of the Spirit is in all goodness and righteousness and truth.

—Eph. 5:8–9

He set the task of sharing his Word before us. To do so, we need to know and understand his Word. Read and study every day. You cannot be light if you don't know light.

Everyone therefore who hears these words of mine and does them, I will liken him to a wise man who built his house on a rock. The rain came down, the floods came, and the winds blew and beat on that house; and it didn't fall, for it was founded on the rock. Everyone who hears these words of mine and doesn't do them will be like a foolish man who built his house on the sand. The rain came down, the floods came, and the winds blew and beat on that house; and it fell—and its fall was great.

—Matt. 7:24–27

---❖---

TURN YOUR
EYES UPON JESUS

*As they went on their way, he entered into a certain village,
and a certain woman named Martha received him into her
house. She had a sister called Mary, who also sat at Jesus' feet,
and heard his word. But Martha was distracted with much
serving, and she came up to him, and said, "Lord, don't you
care that my sister left me to serve alone? Ask her therefore to
help me."*

*Jesus answered her, "Martha, Martha, you are anxious
and troubled about many things, but one thing is needed.
Mary has chosen the good part, which will not be taken away
from her."*

—Luke 10:38–42

*The lamp of the body is the eye. Therefore when your eye is
good, your whole body is also full of light; but when it is evil,
your body also is full of darkness. Therefore see whether the
light that is in you isn't darkness. If therefore your whole body
is full of light, having no part dark, it will be wholly full of
light, as when the lamp with its bright shining gives you light.*

—Luke 11:34–36

"Turn Your Eyes upon Jesus" is a hymn written in 1918 by Helen Howarth Lemmel. Look at the words.

> O soul, are you weary and troubled?
> No light in the darkness you see?
> There's light for a look at the Savior,
> And life more abundant and free!
>
> Refrain: Turn your eyes upon Jesus,
> Look full in His wonderful face,
> And the things of earth will grow strangely dim,
> In the light of His glory and grace.
>
> Through death into life everlasting
> He passed, and we follow Him there;
> O'er us sin no more hath dominion
> For more than conquerors we are!
>
> His Word shall not fail you, He promised;
> Believe Him and all will be well;
> Then go to a world that is dying,
> His perfect salvation to tell!

As I read the words again and again and hear the hymn in my head, the words echo the prayer in my heart. I intentionally and regularly seek more spiritual depth. The program I joined at work called Spiritual Direction set the stage, but many other things have contributed to a palpable feeling of the Spirit within me. The sum total takes me to these words of the song: "And the things of earth will grow strangely dim." The Holy Bible teaches us to seek God, Jesus, and the Holy Spirit.

> *Seek Yahweh and his strength.*
> *Seek his face forever more.*
>
> —1 Chron. 16:11

Now set your heart and your soul to follow Yahweh your God. Arise therefore, and build the sanctuary of Yahweh God, to bring the ark of Yahweh's covenant and the holy vessels of God into the house that is to be built for Yahweh's name.

—1 Chron. 22:19

This verse was written to the nation of Israel as David was preparing to build the temple. Read that verse from a New Testament perspective with each of us as the temple of God. What does that mean for you and the thoughts of your heart?

When you said, "Seek my face,"
my heart said to you, "I will seek your face, Yahweh."

—Ps. 27:8

He made from one blood every nation of men to dwell on all the surface of the earth, having determined appointed seasons, and the boundaries of their dwellings, that they should seek the Lord, if perhaps they might reach out for him and find him, though he is not far from each one of us.

—Acts 17:26–27

Whoever will call on the name of the Lord will be saved.

—Rom. 10:13

Jesus's own words describe the joy of turning your eyes upon him.

I am the bread of life. Whoever comes to me will not be hungry, and whoever believes in me will never be thirsty.

—John 6:35

Again, therefore, Jesus spoke to them, saying, "I am the light of the world. He who follows me will not walk in the darkness, but will have the light of life."

—John 8:12

But turning fully to Jesus comes with a price.

He said to all, "If anyone desires to come after me, let him deny himself, take up his cross, and follow me."
                                                                    —Luke 9:23

The passages opening this chapter demonstrate the words of the hymn's refrain. Mary, Martha, and their brother Lazarus were friends and supporters of Jesus. Martha was providing the requisite hospitality to her visitor, while Mary was fully engaged with Jesus. Martha was concentrating on "the things of earth," while Mary had "turned her eyes upon Jesus." Jesus told Martha that Mary had made the better choice, for she had chosen Jesus and not the world.

In the second passage, Jesus tells us that our eyes are the lamps of our bodies. In other words, what we look at (or turn toward) reflects the condition of our heart. In John, Jesus is identified as the light. If we are turned fully toward Jesus, our eyes reflect his light, "the light of His glory and grace," and there is no room for darkness (the world). But notice what happened to Mary when she focused on Jesus. "The things of earth" grew "strangely dim." I think Mary didn't even notice that Martha was still focused on serving those who had gathered. I think that Mary had room in her thoughts only for Jesus. The New Testament letters support Mary's action.

Don't be conformed to this world, but be transformed by the renewing of your mind, so that you may prove what is the good, well-pleasing, and perfect will of God.
                                                                    —Rom. 12:2

But godliness with contentment is great gain.
                                                                    —1 Tim. 6:6

For our light affliction, which is for the moment, works for us more and more exceedingly an eternal weight of glory, while we don't look at the things which are seen, but at the things which are not seen. For the things which are seen are temporal, but the things which are not seen are eternal.

—2 Cor. 4:17–18

In the past, you were not a people, but now are God's people, who had not obtained mercy, but now have obtained mercy.

   Beloved, I beg you as foreigners and pilgrims, to abstain from fleshly lusts, which war against the soul.

—1 Pet. 2:10–11

For the grace of God has appeared, bringing salvation to all men, instructing us to the intent that, denying ungodliness and worldly lusts, we would live soberly, righteously, and godly in this present age; looking for the blessed hope and appearing of the glory of our great God and Savior, Jesus Christ.

—Titus 2:11–13

Don't love the world or the things that are in the world. If anyone loves the world, the Father's love isn't in him. For all that is in the world, the lust of the flesh, the lust of the eyes, and the pride of life, isn't the Father's, but is the world's. The world is passing away with its lusts, but he who does God's will remains forever.

—1 John 2:15–17

Therefore prepare your minds for action. Be sober, and set your hope fully on the grace that will be brought to you at the revelation of Jesus Christ—as children of obedience, not conforming yourselves according to your former lusts as in your ignorance.

—1 Pet. 1:13–14

Set your mind on the things that are above, not on the things that are on the earth.

—Col. 3:2

Finally, brothers, whatever things are true, whatever things are honorable, whatever things are just, whatever things are pure, whatever things are lovely, whatever things are of good report: if there is any virtue and if there is any praise, think about these things.

—Phil. 4:8

"And the things of earth will grow strangely dim." I find myself moving closer and closer to this cherished ideal. I'm not there yet, but oh, how sweet it feels to be closer! As I devote more of my time each day to prayer using the prayer language, deliberately study and practice forgiveness, increase my giving to my church and other organizations serving God's people, and regularly study God's Word, I find that the cares and worries of the world—things that used to weigh on my mind— fade. I consciously surrender to God's leading and find myself contented. I've learned in a very comforting way that I am part of God's plan.

Rather than going with the flow, I'm part of the flow. I recently watched the John Wayne movie *Rooster Cogburn*. Toward the end of the movie, the characters board a raft, and the river's current carries them downstream. When the current gets rough, the raft hits the rocks and shore. It is tossed and out of control, going wherever the current takes it. The "things of earth" will do that to us if we let them. They will decide our course. But I don't feel out of control in the slightest. The peace of turning my eyes upon Jesus, in all the forms that has taken, makes me feel part of the river's flow, moving with God's purpose to accomplish God's desires, anxious for nothing. *"Therefore don't be anxious for tomorrow, for tomorrow will be anxious for itself. Each day's own evil is sufficient"* (Matt. 6:34). I write all of this to say that if I can experience it, you can too!

Don't lay up treasures for yourselves on the earth, where moth and rust consume, and where thieves break through and steal; but lay up for yourselves treasures in heaven, where neither moth nor rust consume, and where thieves don't break through and steal; for where your treasure is, there your heart will be also.

—Matt. 6:19–21

171

---❖---

ADVENT
EQUALS GRACE

For God so loved the world, that he gave his one and only Son, that whoever believes in him should not perish, but have eternal life.

—John 3:16

The people who walked in darkness have seen a great light.

The light has shined on those who lived in the land of the shadow of death. You have multiplied the nation.
You have increased their joy.

They rejoice before you according to the joy in harvest, as men rejoice when they divide the plunder. For the yoke of his burden, and the staff of his shoulder, the rod of his oppressor, you have broken as in the day of Midian. For all the armor of the armed man in the noisy battle, and the garments rolled in blood, will be for burning, fuel for the fire. For a child is born to us. A son is given to us; and the government will be on his shoulders. His name will be called Wonderful Counselor, Mighty God, Everlasting Father, Prince of Peace. Of the increase of his government and of peace there shall be no end, on David's throne, and on his kingdom, to establish it, and to uphold it with justice and with righteousness from that time on, even forever. The zeal of Yahweh of Armies will perform this.

—Isa. 9:2–7

There were shepherds in the same country staying in the field, and keeping watch by night over their flock. Behold, an angel of the Lord stood by them, and the glory of the Lord shone around them, and they were terrified. The angel said to them, "Don't be afraid, for behold, I bring you good news of great joy which will be to all the people. For there is born to you today, in David's city, a Savior, who is Christ the Lord. This is the sign to you: you will find a baby wrapped in strips of cloth, lying in a feeding trough." Suddenly, there was with the angel a multitude of the heavenly army praising God, and saying,
 "Glory to God in the highest,
  on earth peace, good will toward men."
—Luke 2:8–14

Many traditions celebrate the four Sundays preceding Christmas Day as a season called Advent—*advent* simply means "coming." Traditionally, there are four themes, one for each week: hope, peace, love, and joy. But the true theme for each week, the season of Advent or any other week of the year, is grace.

The prophecy of Jesus's birth as told by Isaiah and the account of Jesus's birth as told by Luke point us to hope, joy, and peace. John 3:16 tells us why God sent his Son to live among us and die for our sins. It was his love. Since God's love is the origin of Advent (the reason for the coming of Christ), let's start there.

Scripture is rich in God's love for us. He sent his Son to die for our sins, not because we are worthy but because he loves us. *"But God commends his own love toward us, in that while we were yet sinners, Christ died for us"* (Rom. 5:8). This verse epitomizes the very definition of grace—the unmerited, unearned favor of God. Additionally, we know that grace is God's nature.

Give thanks to Yahweh, for he is good;
 for his loving kindness endures forever.
—Ps. 136:1

But you, Lord, are a merciful and gracious God,
slow to anger, and abundant in loving kindness and truth.
—Ps. 86:15

See how great a love the Father has given to us, that we should
be called children of God! For this cause the world doesn't
know us, because it didn't know him.
—1 John 3:1

And we know that grace has always been God's nature, in both the Old Testament and New Testament, because God never changes.

Every good gift and every perfect gift is from above, coming
down from the Father of lights, with whom can be no variation,
nor turning shadow.
—James 1:17

For I, Yahweh, don't change.
—Mal. 3:6

But, as with God's grace, we must respond to God's love.

A new commandment I give to you, that you love one another.
Just as I have loved you, you also love one another. By this
everyone will know that you are my disciples, if you have love
for one another.
—John 13:34–35

Beloved, let's love one another, for love is of God; and everyone
who loves has been born of God, and knows God. He who
doesn't love doesn't know God, for God is love.
—1 John 4:7–8

If we call ourselves Christians, we are called to spread that love as Jesus loves us.

Isaiah's prophecy of the Messiah's birth comes after a time of warning to Israel and Judah. Israel had fallen away from worship and service to God. Isaiah was telling them to turn back to the one true God, to serve and follow only him. But Isaiah told them there was hope for the future, for a Messiah would come and bring light to a dark world, lighten the load of his people, and reign forever. Hope for tomorrow was based on Jesus's coming (Advent).

Our hope for tomorrow is based on Jesus's coming into our hearts. Therefore, let us rest in the hope of tomorrow, both in this lifetime and in the eternal life to come.

> *Now may the God of hope fill you with all joy and peace in believing, that you may abound in hope, in the power of the Holy Spirit.*
>
> *I myself am also persuaded about you, my brothers, that you yourselves are full of goodness, filled with all knowledge, able also to admonish others.*
>
> —Rom. 15:13–14

> *Blessed be the God and Father of our Lord Jesus Christ, who according to his great mercy caused us to be born again to a living hope through the resurrection of Jesus Christ from the dead, to an incorruptible and undefiled inheritance that doesn't fade away, reserved in Heaven for you, who by the power of God are guarded through faith for a salvation ready to be revealed in the last time. Wherein you greatly rejoice, though now for a little while, if need be, you have been grieved in various trials, that the proof of your faith, which is more precious than gold that perishes even though it is tested by fire, may be found to result in praise, glory, and honor at the revelation of Jesus Christ.*
>
> —1 Pet. 1:3–7

Let's hold fast the confession of our hope without wavering; for he who promised is faithful.

—Heb. 10:23

Therefore prepare your minds for action. Be sober, and set your hope fully on the grace that will be brought to you at the revelation of Jesus Christ.

—1 Pet. 1:13

Advent equals grace because Jesus brought us hope for an everlasting life with Him.

Luke details Jesus's birth in a beautiful picture of humility, obedience, awe, honor, joy, and peace. The angels announced Jesus's birth to the lowliest of laborers—the shepherds. They were first scared and then overcome with awe, for in Jesus, the world would find peace.

Many translations tell the story of peace "among men," but the earlier translations say peace "toward men." Is there a distinction? I think so. I don't believe the angel's announcement of peace meant an end of strife among nations and peoples. Peace referred to the end of strife between God and sinners through Jesus.

Don't think that I came to send peace on the earth. I didn't come to send peace, but a sword. For I came to set a man at odds against his father, and a daughter against her mother, and a daughter-in-law against her mother-in-law. A man's foes will be those of his own household. He who loves father or mother more than me is not worthy of me; and he who loves son or daughter more than me isn't worthy of me. He who doesn't take his cross and follow after me isn't worthy of me.

—Matt. 10:34–38

In these verses, Jesus explains that a relationship with him ought to be our top priority. By putting him first, we will still have strife in our lives—strife that may even come to the point it separates members of a family. But we will have peace with God and peace in our souls.

Peace I leave with you. My peace I give to you; not as the world gives, I give to you. Don't let your heart be troubled, neither let it be fearful.
—John 14:27

Now may the Lord of peace himself give you peace at all times in all ways. The Lord be with you all.
—2 Thess. 3:16

In nothing be anxious, but in everything, by prayer and petition with thanksgiving, let your requests be made known to God. And the peace of God, which surpasses all understanding, will guard your hearts and your thoughts in Christ Jesus.
—Phil. 4:6–7

You will keep whoever's mind is steadfast in perfect peace,
because he trusts in you.
—Isa. 26:3

Advent equals grace because our peace is in our relationship with Jesus.

Luke explains that the news of Christ's birth would bring great joy to all the people. Joy is the expression of our inner peace, manifested in hope not only for eternity but also for the challenges of this life. It is brought forth from God's love for us. We are joyful because we are surrounded by his grace, for he has saved our souls.

My lips shall shout for joy!
My soul, which you have redeemed, sings praises to you!
—Ps. 71:23

*Whom, not having known, you love. In him, though now you
don't see him, yet believing, you rejoice greatly with joy that
is unspeakable and full of glory, receiving the result of your
faith, the salvation of your souls.*

—1 Pet. 1:8–9

Advent equals grace because the source of our joy and salvation is the
good news of God's Son. Without God's grace, there would be no Son sent
to earth—no Advent. Without God's grace, there would be no hope for
eternity, joy, or peace. Grace is a gift.

*For by grace you have been saved through faith, and that not
of yourselves; it is the gift of God, not of works, that no one
would boast.*

—Eph. 2:8–9

*And if by grace, then it is no longer of works; otherwise grace
is no longer grace. But if it is of works, it is no longer grace;
otherwise work is no longer work.*

—Rom. 11:6

If receiving God's grace were payment for our works, it would be
wages, and we know that *"the wages of sin is death, but the free gift of God
is eternal life in Christ Jesus our Lord"* (Rom. 6:23).

Certainly, Advent equals grace.

I'LL SAVE MINE
FOR LATER

He also said to his disciples, "There was a certain rich man who had a manager. An accusation was made to him that this man was wasting his possessions. He called him, and said to him, 'What is this that I hear about you? Give an accounting of your management, for you can no longer be manager.'

"The manager said within himself, 'What will I do, seeing that my lord is taking away the management position from me? I don't have strength to dig. I am ashamed to beg. I know what I will do, so that when I am removed from management, they may receive me into their houses.' Calling each one of his lord's debtors to him, he said to the first, 'How much do you owe to my lord?' He said, 'A hundred batos of oil.' He said to him, 'Take your bill, and sit down quickly and write fifty.' Then he said to another, 'How much do you owe?' He said, 'A hundred cors of wheat.' He said to him, 'Take your bill, and write eighty.'

"His lord commended the dishonest manager because he had done wisely, for the children of this world are, in their own generation, wiser than the children of the light. I tell you, make for yourselves friends by means of unrighteous mammon, so that when you fail, they may receive you into the eternal tents. He who is faithful in a very little is faithful also in much. He

who is dishonest in a very little is also dishonest in much.
If therefore you have not been faithful in the unrighteous
mammon, who will commit to your trust the true riches? If
you have not been faithful in that which is another's, who will
give you that which is your own? No servant can serve two
masters, for either he will hate the one, and love the other; or
else he will hold to one, and despise the other. You aren't able
to serve God and Mammon."

—Luke 16:1–13

The parable of the unjust steward, in this version called a "manager," can be a bit perplexing on the surface because it appears that the steward is commended for being unjust. But what was he really commended for? For some perspective, note that this parable follows the three parables of the lost returning home—the lost sheep, the lost coin, and the prodigal son. It is followed closely by the parable of the rich man and Lazarus. The common theme in all of them is eternal life. This parable, however, has a bit different flavor from the others. Let's step through it point by point.

The steward had charge of all his master's business. He had been trusted to look out for the best interest of the master like a modern manager, if you will. In a sense, God has done the same thing with us. He has trusted us to carry out his business on earth. Notice also that what the steward managed was not his; it belonged to the master. And what we have is not ours either; it belongs to our Master.

At some point, the steward would be called to account for his actions. When he realized the accounting would happen soon, he realized he had to do something and do it right away. Do we realize that someday we will be called to account for our actions as well? While we don't know the day, it could be soon. Maybe we should take that knowledge seriously and do something about it right now.

The steward said, *"I don't have strength to dig. I am ashamed to beg."* It could be that he was either physically weak, uneducated in other means of work, or just too lazy or proud to do manual labor. I wonder how many of us are uneducated in God's work, just too lazy, or too proud to speak up for him when we have an opportunity to do so.

The steward had been living for the moment with little thought for his future, assuming the position he had was secure. When his position was coming to an end, he decided to continue in his dishonesty (dishonesty leads to dishonesty) by using his position to secure his future. He sought to make friends by canceling their debt to his master. Here is the real lesson in this parable. The steward was not commended for his continued dishonesty. He was commended by his master for using what he had to secure his future.

As Jesus said, the world works diligently and shrewdly to continue after worldly things. We are to work diligently and wisely to continue after godly things. As the steward used his position and influence to secure his future, we are to use our resources (money, position, influence, talents) to demonstrate our already secured future. We are to be about the Father's work. How do we do that? We "make friends" by making today better for others, not dishonestly as the steward did by discounting debt but by providing for those in need—helping the sick, lonely, hungry, cold, and unsaved among us. In other words, we need to give to God's kingdom with money, time, talent, and abilities.

Certainly, several of Jesus's teachings centered on our relationship to money—the rich young ruler, for example. Money must not possess us; it is merely a tool for our use. In the passage above, money is called "unrighteous." This is not a reference to how the money was gained but rather that the allure of money is unrighteous and dishonest. It may look promising, but putting our hope in money (the world) is false hope.

Rather than waiting until we have "enough" to give our tithes and offerings, we need to begin giving now. *"He who is faithful in a very little is faithful also in much. He who is dishonest in a very little is also dishonest in much. If therefore you have not been faithful in the unrighteous mammon, who will commit to your trust the true riches?"* (Luke 16:10–11). In the text, money is alluded to as "very little." "True riches" reference the other blessings from God. In other words, if you can be faithful with the small things (money), you can be trusted with bigger talents, responsibilities, and blessings. God will use you as far as you allow him to, but he must know your heart. How you spend the money he has put in your stewardship is a great indicator of your heart, *"for where your treasure is, there your heart will be also"* (Matt. 6:21).

Are you missing some of God's blessings (not just monetary) because you aren't using what he has already given you to build his kingdom? Since I was young and mowing yards for money, I have given to my church, but I didn't always give my "first fruits." What I gave wasn't always based on the full blessing (net pay as opposed to gross pay, for example). We now tithe based on the gross pay we receive, along with any other money that may come our way—and for some of that, we may have already paid a tithe (insurance reimbursements, tax refunds, and so forth). Additionally, we give to other organizations we feel are, by extension, doing God's work. I have found a notable difference in my internal peace, desire to serve Him, and, yes, my finances since we have elevated our giving. Again, I relate this only because if I can experience this, so can you!

> *But seek first God's Kingdom and his righteousness; and all these things will be given to you as well.*
>
> —Matt. 6:33

---❖---

WORK OUT YOUR
OWN SALVATION

So then, my beloved, even as you have always obeyed, not only in my presence, but now much more in my absence, work out your own salvation with fear and trembling. For it is God who works in you both to will and to work, for his good pleasure.

—Phil. 2:12–13

In his letter to the Philippians, Paul offers great wisdom on a variety of topics. This meaning of *"work out your own salvation"* can go in two different directions. In several verses preceding and following this verse, Paul hints at the meaning of the word *work* as "do." In other words, go act upon what our salvation encourages (please read the entire letter for more depth). But the meaning may also be "build," as in building the details of our own salvation and not leaning on someone else's. I'd like to look at both meanings.

Before we can *"work out"* our own salvation by *doing*, we must *"work out"* our own salvation by *building*—first a foundation and then a full structure. We can't build our house on someone else's property, but we can seek help from the master builders around us. *"According to the grace of God which was given to me, as a wise master builder I laid a foundation, and another builds on it. But let each man be careful how he builds on it"* (1 Cor. 3:10). The foundation is accepting Jesus as Lord and Savior.

That if you will confess with your mouth that Jesus is Lord, and believe in your heart that God raised him from the dead, you will be saved.

—Rom. 10:9

No one can come to me unless the Father who sent me draws him, and I will raise him up in the last day.

—John 6:44

God will draw us to himself, and he wants to draw all of us. For some, like me, this process can be subtle, maybe so subtle we don't realize it. As I've said, I was raised in church. I feel the "land" my structure is built on was bought and paid for by those who helped shape me during my young years. But steadily over time, I have added my own understanding. I've developed a relationship that I own and understand. I've studied and considered. I've sought his will and surrendered mine.

But you remain in the things which you have learned and have been assured of, knowing from whom you have learned them. From infancy, you have known the holy Scriptures which are able to make you wise for salvation through faith, which is in Christ Jesus. Every Scripture is God-breathed and profitable for teaching, for reproof, for correction, and for instruction in righteousness, that each person who belongs to God may be complete, thoroughly equipped for every good work.

—2 Tim. 3:14–17

For some, this process may begin with a dramatic event, a miraculous conversion of sorts. But after the emotion of the situation, you must continue to grow and develop your own relationship with the Father.

Therefore the Lord Yahweh says, "Behold, I lay in Zion for a foundation a stone, a tried stone, a precious cornerstone of a sure foundation. He who believes shall not act hastily."

—Isa. 28:16

*But grow in the grace and knowledge of our Lord and Savior
Jesus Christ. To him be the glory both now and forever. Amen.*
—2 Pet. 3:18

Others may fall somewhere in between. But know this: If you feel
you have not been drawn by God, *"Ask, and it will be given you. Seek, and
you will find. Knock, and it will be opened for you. For everyone who asks
receives. He who seeks finds. To him who knocks it will be opened"* (Matt.
7:7–8).

Here is the goal in "working out" our own salvation by building. We
should strain (not with difficulty, but with desire and energy) to build
an intimate relationship with God and Jesus through the Holy Spirit,
engaging our full heart, soul, and mind as Jesus taught. From that
intimate relationship, we will find a confidence for the trials of life that
most certainly will come.

*Seeing that his divine power has granted to us all things that
pertain to life and godliness, through the knowledge of him who
called us by his own glory and virtue, by which he has granted
to us his precious and exceedingly great promises; that through
these you may become partakers of the divine nature, having
escaped from the corruption that is in the world by lust. Yes, and
for this very cause adding on your part all diligence, in your faith
supply moral excellence; and in moral excellence, knowledge; and
in knowledge, self-control; and in self-control perseverance; and
in perseverance godliness; and in godliness brotherly affection;
and in brotherly affection, love. For if these things are yours and
abound [if you have an intimate relationship], they make you to
not be idle or unfruitful in the knowledge of our Lord Jesus Christ.*
—2 Pet. 1:3–8

*For though we walk in the flesh, we don't wage war according
to the flesh; for the weapons of our warfare are not of the flesh,
but mighty before God to the throwing down of strongholds,*

throwing down imaginations and every high thing that is exalted against the knowledge of God and bringing every thought into captivity to the obedience of Christ, and being in readiness to avenge all disobedience when your obedience is made full.

—2 Cor. 10:3–6

We are saved through grace. Without the grace of the Father, I'm confident that the events of Noah and his ark would have been repeated in some fashion multiple times throughout history. But God created us in his own image. He created each of us to have an intimate relationship with him because he loves us. His love for us forced him to offer us grace; there was no other way for Him to express love. Through grace, he offered his Son as the atonement for our sins.

We could stop with salvation only, but why would we want to? That isn't God's best for us, nor is it his will. He asks for his love to be expressed in our lives, and he asks us to *"work out"* our salvation—to make it visible to others. Jesus gives us this instruction:

Jesus answered them, . . . "Don't work for the food which perishes, but for the food which remains to eternal life, which the Son of Man will give to you. For God the Father has sealed him."

They said therefore to him, "What must we do, that we may work the works of God?"

Jesus answered them, "This is the work of God, that you believe in him whom he has sent."

—John 6:26–29

I must work the works of him who sent me while it is day. The night is coming, when no one can work.

—John 9:4

John and Jesus's brother James added more instruction under the influence of the Holy Spirit.

By this we know love, because he laid down his life for us. And we ought to lay down our lives for the brothers.

—1 John 3:16

Yes, a man will say, "You have faith, and I have works." Show me your faith without works, and I will show you my faith by my works.

—James 2:18

Who is wise and understanding among you? Let him show by his good conduct that his deeds are done in gentleness of wisdom.

—James 3:13

Paul continues.

For we are his workmanship, created in Christ Jesus for good works, which God prepared before that we would walk in them.

—Eph. 2:10

Therefore, my beloved brothers, be steadfast, immovable, always abounding in the Lord's work, because you know that your labor is not in vain in the Lord.

—1 Cor. 15:58

In all things show yourself an example of good works. In your teaching, show integrity, seriousness, incorruptibility, and soundness of speech that can't be condemned, that he who opposes you may be ashamed, having no evil thing to say about us.

—Titus 2:7–8

But let each man examine his own work, and then he will have reason to boast in himself, and not in someone else. For each man will bear his own burden.

—Gal. 6:4–5

Work out your own salvation. Build it, and then do it!

This is eternal life, that they should know you, the only true God, and him whom you sent, Jesus Christ.

—John 17:3

Amen!

www.ingramcontent.com/pod-product-compliance
Lightning Source LLC
Chambersburg PA
CBHW062215080426
42734CB00010B/1900